# FRENCH COUNTRY COOKING

# FRENCH
# COUNTRY
# COOKING

## Ann Hughes-Gilbey

CHARTWELL
BOOKS, INC.

All recipes serve four unless
otherwise stated.

Cooking times may vary slightly
depending on the individual oven.

Always preheat the oven or broiler
to the specified temperature.

To avoid constant repetition of
basic information certain recipes
and preparation techniques are
marked with an asterisk. Full
information about these terms can
be found in the Reference File on
p. 132. Explanations of certain
technical terms can be found in the
Glossary on p. 141.

*I dedicate this book to my darling husband
Denis, who died before he could finish the
photography.*

RIGHT *Making butter on a Normandy farm*

FRONTISPIECE *Fruit and vegetables on sale in
a market*

Copyright © Ann Hughes-Gilbey 1983
First published in 1983 by Artus Books

This 1994 edition published by
Chartwell Books Inc.
A division of Book Sales Inc.
114 Northfield Avenue, Raritan Center,
Edison, New Jersey 08818

This edition produced for sale in the U.S.A.,
its territories and dependencies only.

ISBN 0 7858 0044 1

Printed and bound in Italy

# Contents

# Introduction

French regional cuisine has evolved from the cooking of the country housewife through the ages. When roads were poor and public transport nil, her lifestyle was incredibly busy – which meant that shopping expeditions were major events taking place, as a rule, only once or twice a year. On these trips she would stock up with imperishable items for her pantry, buying them with any money left over from such essential purchases as farm implements and basic clothing.

For the rest of the year she had to rely entirely on produce she grew or raised herself, or which she could buy or barter from any other households within easy reach. With no refrigeration, any of her own produce which was surplus to immediate requirements had to be canned, salted, dried, cured or otherwise preserved for future use (pp. 108–15). In addition she made full use of Nature's bounty, collecting fruit, flowers, leaves, roots and fungi from the fields and forests – both for the domestic animals and for her family (pp. 100–7).

People who lived in villages were luckier than those in isolated farms: there were neighbors to help with the chores associated with harvesting fruit, killing a pig and so on. Such communities, however small, meant the availability of more varied produce: one could exchange some eggs for a cow's milk cheese, for example, or chickens for rabbits, wine for honey, kids for geese, or perhaps fruit for butter or cream – and there might even be a nearby mill to grind corn and walnuts.

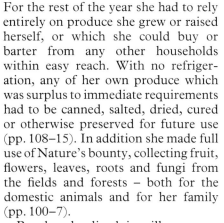

Thrift was an essential part of the country housewife's "kitchen equipment," but necessity begat ingenuity and she became adept at combining unlikely or unpromising ingredients to make an enjoyable meal. (An important influence in this respect was an order of nuns known as *menettes*. From the eighteenth century these dedicated women were trained in household crafts and sent out into the world to act as servants; their kitchen skills were said to have added *noblesse* to peasant cooking, making it more truly appetizing.)

Though some of the food the housewife used may seem to be what we might consider delicacies, it was everyday fare to many families: sole or salmon was free to the fisherman, cream to the cowman, *foie gras* to anyone who raised geese, game to the woodsman (or poacher). Thousands of households made their own wine and had access to spirits – delectable fruit or berry brandies or, at the very least, *marc*. (Made by distilling the grape residue after wine-pressing, this could be fiery and rather tasteless on its own but was deliciously transformed when used to preserve fruit.)

Because she shared the field work of the farm with her husband, as well as raising the children and cleaning the house, tending the chickens, rabbits, goats and cow if there was one, the country wife's cooking techniques were honed to a fine art: either a meal was made in as short a time as possible before eating, or it was prepared in advance and left to cook in a pot over the fire (or in the oven if she had one), needing only the occasional stir – or addition of the next batch of ingredients – when she happened to be passing through the kitchen or could snatch a few moments from her other work.

Another characteristic of this type of cooking was (and still is) its versatility. With no time for precise measuring, amounts of ingredients were dictated by mood or by supply: when the sorrel was over, one used chard or cabbage; if there were too few fresh beans, dried ones were increased; extra root vegetables could compensate for a paucity of potatoes, and so on. Similarly, when

her supply of town-bought wheat flour was finished, rye, corn, potato or even chestnut flour could be substituted; a handful of currants might suffice if the sugar was running low; when the ham or bacon became too dry for anything but boiling in soup, eggs or extra cheese could take its place – perhaps with some herbs or a pinch of spice added to make up for any lost flavor.

So, although quantities are specified in the majority of recipes in this book, feel free to alter them after the first time if you feel like a change. In soups and stews particularly, the proportions of ingredients are far from critical, so change them if it suits your taste, pocket or pantry better. Unlike classic *haute cuisine*, there is no "right" or "wrong" way in bourgeois cooking, which is infinitely variable. (You'll find a number of informal recipes in these pages, giving suggestions for ingredients and cooking methods, to enable you to make your own versions.)

Regional cuisine naturally draws some of its character from the produce most prevalent in the locality, and this applies especially to cooking fat. This plays an enormously important part in influencing the flavor of cooked food – both as an intrinsic ingredient and as a cooking medium. Extraordinarily varied through rural France, its choice is another hangover from the days when commodities did not travel far from their places of origin.

In Provence and westward along the stony *garrigues* through the Rhône delta and Languedoc into Spain, the

OPPOSITE *Autumn picnic, Autun, Bourgogne*

6

land was too harsh for cattle, so there was no cow's milk or butter. Olives flourished in the barren soil, so olive oil was used for all culinary purposes and, together with those other famous products of the region – tomatoes, garlic and herbs – it gives unmistakable "personality" to southern cooking.

The lusher countryside of what has been called "the golden crescent" – curving up from Bordeaux through Poitou, Normandy and the North, Anjou, Touraine and the Ile de France, and down again through Burgundy to Franche-Comté – supports dairy herds in abundance. Here, understandably, butter is king of the kitchen. It rules in Savoy and Dauphiné as well – surprisingly, until you remember the splendid high-altitude pastures: though the cows spend only their summers up there, they benefit enough to produce some of France's most sought-after cheeses and richest butter.

The rest is "pig-in-the-middle" country: neither rich nor poor, it is equally unsuitable for olives and for dairy herds. It stretches from the Landes through Périgord and Rouergue to the highlands of the Massif Central, with a detached outpost in Alsace. For a number of reasons the inhabitants here sensibly turned to rearing those economical creatures, pigs and geese: raised by old-fashioned methods, they cost little to feed, gain weight quickly, produce excellent meat and plenty of spare fat. Goose fat is particularly fragrant and some country folk still use no other – even for sweet pastries. (It plays an important role in the preparation of the famous *confits*, see p. 108.) Conveniently enough, these fats are wonderfully complementary to the beans (cooked both fresh and dried), lentils, potatoes and cabbage which are native to the same areas.

Perhaps the luckiest regions are those which use all these cooking media impartially: the Pays Basque and Navarre right through the Pyrenean foothills into eastern Languedoc.

Researching provincial cuisine in the field is great fun, but not as easy as you might expect. Plenty of people are willing to discuss local delicacies with you, embroidering their discourse with

mouth-watering tales of remembered meals from their childhood days – but it is surprising at first how often you will find that a restaurant's *specialités maison* come from another region altogether. Reflection provides two answers to this paradox.

First: unless it is in a mainly tourist area (these are never particularly rich in genuine regional cooking), a restaurant's main trade comes from the local people. The natives, the *patron* believes, possibly with some justification, know all they want to know about local dishes and probably eat them often at home. When they go out for a meal they want a treat, something different, maybe even a bit exotic. (The exceptions are Brittany with its seafood, and Dordogne, whose best-known specialties are *foie gras* and truffles. Once true peasant fare – the one was raised in your own backyard, the other was free if you knew where to look for it – these delicacies are now so expensive as to be in the high *luxe* class, and local diners as well as visitors seek them out in the restaurants when they want to celebrate.)

Second: the traditional life-cycle of the average chef. Having discovered his vocation, he goes for training, probably in Paris. Then he takes a job, ideally in a well-known establishment under a famous chef, to learn more kitchen techniques and business methods; this may be anywhere in France. When he decides to open a restaurant of his own,

the odds are that the place he can find and afford at that moment may also not be in his home territory (though it is noticeable that many successful chefs will return "home" eventually). So through much of his working life he may be specializing in dishes from the area where he spent his apprentice years, or nostalgically recreating the meals of his extreme youth.

Historical research is even more difficult – but fascinating. Old cookbooks in every language are cheerfully vague. The metric system of weights and measures officially came into force after the French Revolution, but the old terms persisted for another century and a half in some country districts. The same bad roads which kept peasants tied to their own *pays* meant that these terms varied from one district to another – and, incidentally, ensured that French remained a foreign language to all but a few town dwellers until quite recent times; countrymen continued to speak their local patois.

A book of mine, found years ago by my mother in a second-hand bookshop in Brittany, has been neatly rebound in linen by some careful French *ménagère*, its front carrying the legend *Livre de Cuisine* inked on with a spiky nib. From its type and layout it appears to have been printed just before or immediately after the First World War, but its style and content suggest that it's an unrevised reprint from the 1850s or earlier.

These old cookbooks are liberally

sprinkled with *pintes, quarts, onces* (for both dry and liquid ingredients) and *livres*. (A *livre* – from Latin *libra* like our lb – was a money unit in France until 1877, and is often used as a half-kilogram weight for food even today.) Other intriguing measures include a *litron* (one sixteenth of a bushel), a *poisson* (of milk – perhaps a "splash"), a *ligne* (an unidentified length). In one recipe we are instructed to roll some forcemeat out to the thickness of a "6-franc *écu*" and, in another, to add a *setier* of cream to a sauce; as the only meanings I can find for *setier* are a bushel or something approaching two gallons, I doubt if this is right!

French food is an endlessly absorbing subject, in which our interest was aroused less by the fabulous *haute cuisine* meals of great restaurants than by a series of motoring vacations in France. The delights of exploring this ancient and beautiful country are significantly enhanced by those of sampling its superb food, wines and cheeses.

Apart from the pleasure of passing on just a little of what we have learned about these traditions, I hope that this book may help you to increase your own enjoyment of cooking. (In a way, the greatest compliment would be not to need the book after a time because it will have shown you how to develop your own creative cookery.)

Enjoy your cooking – and *bon appétit*!

# Notes on Ingredients

*Bacon* See Ham

*Bread* Country bread in France today is generally made with white flour – and some of the loaves are enormous! To keep it fresh longer, the leavening agent is not *levure* (baker's yeast) but *levain*: a soft, yeasty dough mixture kept from the previous day's baking – the same as the old American cowboy's "sourdough." Consider brown flour's stronger flavor before substituting it for white flour.

*Bread crumbs* always mean crumbs freshly made from day-old bread.

*Cheese* The recipes in this book were originally made with regional French cheeses whose names have been omitted as they are not universally available outside France. Generally speaking, "hard" cheeses for grating – or for slicing to melt – are of the Gruyère type; soft ones are *fromage frais* (like homemade or curd or cream cheese beaten up to lightness). "Semi-

soft" denotes Cheddar-*type* cheeses used when set but not hardened; cheeses with a slightly soft "springy" texture, like Pont l'Evêque or St Paulin, fall into this category.

Many bulk cheeses sold as Cheddar are not good for cooking – they are often already sweating under hermetic wraps, have not dried out or matured and sometimes separate greasily when melted. "Real", sharp Cheddar, properly matured, is excellent for the hard-cheese recipes.

*Cream* Originally skimmed off the milk from your own cows. Today's substitute, *crème fraîche*★, replaces tastes and characteristics removed by pasteurization, but satisfactory results may be obtained by using *heavy cream* instead. For economy's sake, *light cream* may be used *provided it is not cooked after it has been added.* Remember that light cream will thin a mixture where heavy would probably thicken it. See also *yogurt.*

*Fat for cooking* Different districts habitually used the fat most readily available locally (see Introduction). With solid fats, by all means substitute whatever you would normally use for the purpose in hand. The flavor of good-quality olive oil is often important to a dish and this is indicated in the recipe.

*Fat for dressings* Vinaigrette dressings★ are particularly good if made with walnut oil or good quality olive oil; the latter is also best for mayonnaise★.

BELOW *Herbs in a Provence Market*

*Flour,* unless otherwise stated, denotes all-purpose white flour, though no doubt the original recipes would have been made with a sort of coarse-ground "wholewheat" type, or rye, potato, corn – or occasionally even chestnut – flour.

*Game* Wild birds and animals may be weighed "dead" or "dressed" – and, in any case, one cannot always command a specific weight. For this reason the weights may be omitted from recipes. If you're in any doubt, tell your supplier how many you wish to feed and let him advise you.

*Ham, Bacon, Salt Pork* Thousands of households cured or salted their own pork and many regions still specialize in dried and/or smoked ham – *jambon de pays* – which, like Parma ham, is exquisite sliced thinly to eat raw. In French country cooking it is also extensively used to add savor, but may be replaced with bacon or ordinary ham: for maximum flavor choose a smoked or high-cure ham or bacon, rather than a mild one. Bacon may be substituted for salt pork if preferred.

*Herbs* It is always best to use *fresh* herbs where possible (many people grow their own – even in window boxes). Properly dried herbs are excellent (except in a few specified cases) and respond to a brief rubbing on the palm of your hand before being added to the cookpot; this helps to release their flavor. Old dried herbs taste bitter and dusty and are worse than useless. Contrary to what you'd expect, you need considerably less dried herb than fresh.

*Nutmeg* Always buy whole nuts and grate them when required (to preserve their flavor).

*Pepper* Use freshly ground wherever possible. Black is most commonly used, white is preferable only where the dish is very pale and might be marred by dark specks, or where its taste is too delicate for the robust flavor of black.

*Rice* Long-grain types (e.g. Patna, Carolina) are best where grains need to be separate; otherwise use whatever you normally would. Remember to add 20–25 minutes to cooking time if substituting brown rice.

*Salt* Originally *gros sel* (sea salt, kosher salt). Except where otherwise stated, any type of salt may be used in recipes.

*Sugar* in France today is nearly always white. For my taste, brown has a better flavor and adds color to caramel, etc. It may be substituted for white except where its color and taste might be a positive disadvantage – e.g. in wine syrups or custards, or with delicate items like almonds or pale fruits.

*Vanilla* Wherever possible (i.e. when it can be infused in a liquid ingredient) do use a vanilla bean; this can be wiped clean and re-used several times. Otherwise choose real vanilla extract, not synthetic flavoring. The best way to store beans is in a closed jar of sugar – which quickly becomes the always useful *vanilla sugar.*

*Wine* There is little point in using fine French château-bottled vintages in cooking, but do use wines which you find pleasant to drink (there's often enough left from the cooking to serve with the finished meal). Plenty of reasonably priced domestic wines are suitable. Naturally, you should choose full-bodied wines with game or dark meats, lighter ones with chicken or desserts; unless stated, do use *dry* wine (whether red or white) with savory dishes.

*Note* If a fish recipe calls for a small quantity of dry white wine and, for any reason, this is not available, a *dry white vermouth* may be substituted.

*Yogurt* has a slight tendency to separate when cooked but, with common sense, it may be substituted for cream in some recipes; it is generally not suitable for sauces. Always beat yogurt to a smooth cream before adding it.

# Soupes et Potages

## ALL MANNER OF SOUPS

Apart from "broiled" (more probably burnt!) meat, soup must have been one of the first known cooked meals. Given water and fire to heat it, there is virtually no limit to what you can transform into soup. In dire hardship the ingredients might once have been only wild or gleaned grain, fruits, fungi, roots or greenery but, if a household could grow its own vegetables, these were used as the basis for all soups. Way back, country people made their own bread in communal bakehouses: it was not very good, but it added welcome body and sustenance to their soups, and the addition of meat, often home-cured pork, was a luxury that improved soups out of all recognition.

For centuries soup was the main – and often sole – content of the European peasant's meals. Even today, French countrymen don't consider they have had a proper meal unless it started with soup; some families still have it three times a day.

Whether as elegant appetizer, light meal or appetite dampener for dieters, soup is delightfully easy to make and; with a little imagination, one hardly needs a recipe. But since so many delicious soups have evolved from simple beginnings, a few basic recipes are set down here to give impetus to your own ingenuity.

The simplest *potages* are the Bread Soups. These are made by pouring a well-flavored stock, with or without chopped vegetables, into a tureen full of bread scraps and leaving it to soak in a warm place, adding more liquid from time to time as it becomes absorbed. ("Eiderdown Soup" was a common dish: a double quantity was made in the morning for lunch and supper, and after lunch the earthenware pot of leftover soup was slid into heaped bedding to keep warm until ready to serve for an evening meal.)

For a complete supper or luncheon dish, add cheese, thus:

# Soupe au Fromage

## BREAD AND CHEESE SOUP

Make or heat up 7 cups well-flavored stock* or thin soup, containing chopped cooked vegetables. Cover the bottom of a large ovenproof bowl or tureen with about 10 slices of lightly toasted bread. Shred ½ lb hard cheese (2 cups), and sprinkle some of this over the bread; ladle on some of the soup, distributing the vegetables evenly. Repeat with more bread, cheese and soup until the container is nearly full (you'll need to keep adding extra stock). Finish with a generous layer of cheese and brown in a fairly hot oven or under the broiler. Add more stock at least once – use a funnel or pour it carefully under the edge to keep the top crisp. Serve each person with a solid ladleful moistened with spare stock from the tureen.

Versions of the above come from every hard-cheese region of France, and variations are endless. What the English think of as Classic French Onion Soup is usually called a *gratinée* in France: chopped onions, cooked in stock, with slices of bread-and-cheese floated on top and then broiled. In Gascony, home of fourth Musketeer d'Artagnan, it's called *Gratinée des Mousquetaires*; the slightly thickened soup is flavored with white wine, and Roquefort cheese is used.

A less solid *soupe au fromage* can be made by thinning a white roux with stock, milk or white wine. Plenty of shredded cheese is added, and more liquid if necessary. Seasoned with salt, pepper and nutmeg or mustard, it's sometimes enriched with a liaison of egg yolks and cream and usually served with a garnish of parsley or garlicky croûtons.

OPPOSITE *Laruns a Pyrenean village*
RIGHT *Soupe au Fromage, a very filling bread and cheese soup with vegetables*

Ripe tomatoes are abundant in high summer, especially in Roussillon, where they make a soup of Catalan ancestry.

# Potage à la Tomate

## TOMATO SOUP

Finely chop a large Spanish onion and soften it gently in 3 tbsp olive oil in a large pan. When transparent, add 2 tbsp roughly chopped celery leaves and heart plus a bouquet garni (or sprig of basil, 2 bay leaves, small bunch of parsley and 2 sprigs of thyme tied in a bundle). Skin, seed and chop roughly 2 lbs ripe tomatoes and add them to the pan, together with salt, pepper and 1 tsp or so of sugar. Add 1–2 cloves crushed garlic too.

Cover generously with water or chicken stock* and simmer the tomatoes to a pulp. Remove bouquet or herbs, squeezing out all liquid, and mill, sieve or liquidize. Check seasoning and serve, either hot with fried garlicky croûtons or cold garnished with chopped parsley or chives (in this case add a bit more seasoning).

Tomato soups similar to this play their part in local customs. For instance, after a wedding in Quercy, some of the guests (no longer quite sober) would accompany the newlyweds up to their room for a nuptial supper of soup and crackers and – if they were lucky – champagne. This may not sound too much of an ordeal, but the soup was sometimes fiercely over-peppered. Though the bride was usually let off after one spoonful, the groom's more ribald friends would not leave him till he'd downed a whole bowlful.

A tomato soup with extra "body" is often made in the southern half of the country. Naturally, as one moves further south, different herbs are available, such as savory and basil, both of which can be used for this soup.

OPPOSITE *Clockwise from top: Tomato Soup, Spring Soup and an unusual Garlic Soup*

# Soupe à la Tomate et aux Haricots

## TOMATO AND BEAN SOUP
SERVES 5–6

1 lb (about 2⅓ cups) *dried navy beans*
*bouquet garni*
1½ lbs *ripe tomatoes, skinned, seeded and chopped roughly*
1–2 *medium-size onions, chopped*
2 tbsp *pork or goose fat, or oil*
3 *garlic cloves, finely chopped*
4–5 *slices bacon, chopped*
2 tbsp *tomato paste*
*salt and pepper*
2–3 tbsp *chopped parsley*

Soak the beans overnight, drain and cook in 1½–2 quarts of fresh unsalted water with the bouquet garni until almost tender. Soften the tomatoes and onions to a pulp in the fat or oil, together with the garlic, bacon and tomato paste, then add them to the cooked beans. Season to taste – the parsley may be added now for flavor or before serving as a garnish – then cover and cook for 50–60 minutes.

There's a famous garlic soup called *aigo boullido* – provençal for "boiled water" – and *"l'aigo boullido sauvo la vido"* ("boiled water saves your life") is a local proverb. This soup is traditionally good for upset stomachs – and standard fare for post-feast days!

Most other garlic soups belong to the *tourain* or *tourin* category (*tourins* are the white threads formed by stirring egg whites into boiling soup).

# Tourain Blanchi à l'Ail

## GARLIC SOUP

6 *or more garlic cloves, finely chopped*
1 tbsp *pork or goose fat*
1 tbsp *flour*
1½ quarts *chicken or veal stock**
1 *egg, separated*
1–2 tsp *vinegar*
*salt and pepper*

Fry the garlic very gently in the melted fat until just golden. Stir in the flour to make a white roux, then slowly add the stock, stirring all the time to avoid lumps. Simmer for 30 minutes.

Add the egg white, whisking so that it separates into hair-thin threads as it cooks.

Beat the yolk with the vinegar and a splash of cold water. Take the soup off the heat. Stir a ladleful into the yolk mix, then incorporate this back into the rest of the soup. Season and serve.

For a variation in color and flavor the stock may include puréed tomatoes or green vegetables, in which case the amount of garlic should be slightly reduced.

There are vegetable soups for all seasons.

# Soupe de Printemps

## SPRING SOUP
SERVES 6–8

By April, the Basques are picking their first crops of beans, peas and early new potatoes, and lettuce and kohlrabi need thinning out. It is these young vegetables that give this early-season soup its delectable flavor.

1 lb *new potatoes, scraped and sliced into ½ inch rounds*
2 quarts *light chicken stock**
*bouquet garni (ideally of thyme, parsley and marjoram)*
*salt and pepper*
1 lb *lima or fava beans, green beans or snow peas, stripped or broken into chunks, or shelled peas*
1 lb *lettuce thinnings or similar very young greens, shredded*
1 tbsp *vinegar*

Put the potatoes into the stock, bring to a boil, add the bouquet garni and seasoning and simmer for 15 minutes. Add the beans or peas and cook for another 5–10 minutes (20 minutes if using snow peas), then add the young greens. Cover and cook gently for another 6 minutes. Just before serving, stir in the vinegar.

13

*Pistou* is the provençal word for basil. In ancient times this was a royal plant and in the Middle Ages it was considered effective against sciatica and snake-bite! Even in hot Provence it is only a summer herb and must be used fresh for this soup – a real evocation of blazing sunny days.

# Soupe au Pistou

## VEGETABLE SOUP WITH BASIL
SERVES 6–8

½ cup *dried navy beans*
½ cup *dried red kidney beans*
¾ lb *green beans, chopped roughly or sliced*
½ lb *potatoes, peeled and diced*
½ lb *tomatoes, skinned and chopped roughly*
2–2½ quarts *chicken stock*★
*salt and pepper*
¾ cup *small-size pasta (optional)*
4–6 *garlic cloves*
*small handful fresh basil leaves, chopped*
6 tbsp *olive oil*
1 *egg yolk*
*about* 1 cup *grated Parmesan or other hard cheese*

Soak the dried beans overnight. Cook them for 20 minutes in fresh, unsalted water; drain. Put them in a pan with the other vegetables, cover with the stock and cook for 35–40 minutes. Season.

Add the pasta and cook for a further 10 minutes or until it is *al dente*. (As this soup is closely related to Italian minestrone, pasta is essential to purists, but omit it if you don't like it.)

Meanwhile pound the garlic and basil with 2 tbsp oil to make a paste; add the egg yolk. Drizzle in the remaining oil in small quantities, stirring steadily, as for a mayonnaise★.

Thin the basil sauce with a ladleful of the vegetable *bouillon*. Just before serving stir this back into the soup, off the heat. Either stir in the cheese or serve it separately.

RIGHT *Soupe au Pistou, a minestrone-like vegetable soup into which is stirred a rich blend of fresh basil and olive oil*

Soups became heartier in autumn's cooler weather – more cheese, ham or bacon were included for extra protein. In olden times ham and bacon were home-cured; by autumn, the previous winter's stocks were becoming scrappy and hard, so boiling them up in the soup made them more edible, as well as improving the soup's flavor.

Grain and grape harvesting both brought extra hungry mouths to the table, and as many ingredients as possible went into the soup. To my mind, the following soup of mixed vegetables with ham and cheese is the archetypal French vegetable soup – provided you pour it onto generous helpings of bread!

# Soupe d'Automne

## AUTUMN SOUP
### SERVES 5–6 AS AN ENTIRE LIGHT MEAL

½ cup *dried navy beans*
2 *carrots, scraped and chopped roughly*
2 *medium-size potatoes, peeled and diced*
2 *zucchini, sliced*
2 *leeks, sliced*
½ lb *green beans, chopped*
1 cup *peeled, seeded and diced pumpkin*
*bouquet garni*
3–4 *black peppercorns*
*salt*
½ lb *ham in a single piece*
1 *ham hock*
1 cup *shredded cheese*

Soak the dried beans overnight; drain. Put in a large pan with the other vegetables, the bouquet garni, peppercorns and salt and cover with 1½ quarts of fresh water; bring to a boil. Add the ham and ham hock, bring back to a boil and skim carefully. Turn down the heat, half cover and simmer for 1½ hours. Take out the ham and hock and chop the ham into bite-size pieces. Return these to the soup and check seasoning. Serve, handing the cheese separately.

*RIGHT Soupe d'Automne, with Provençal Pumpkin Soup (below)*

Pumpkin, a supporting ingredient in the last recipe, is the star of many autumnal *potages*, giving them body, flavor and a beautiful warm color. In fact all pumpkin soups can be made an even more spectacular color by adding a few tomatoes or a spoonful of tomato paste. The simplest soups are merely pumpkin pieces cooked in a little butter and water until pulpy and then puréed; milk, more butter and seasonings are stirred in, along with a touch of sugar to bring out the flavor.

In Savoy they dust the top with shredded cheese; in Franche-Comté it's thickened with tapioca and enriched with an egg-and-cream liaison. In Provence they sweeten it with onions – like this:

# Soupe des Maures

## PROVENÇAL PUMPKIN SOUP

Fry 3–4 large chopped onions in a little oil until well browned. Add an equal quantity of chopped pumpkin and rather less of cooked navy beans; cook in 1 quart of stock★ until tender (about 15 minutes). Purée, then thin as desired with more stock (no milk used here; Provence had no cows to speak of). Cook for another few minutes, adding a handful of pasta if liked. When the pasta is *al dente*, check seasoning and serve.

In October came the walnuts – at least in certain regions – and free for those lucky enough to own trees. As befits their prized status, walnuts make an unusual soup, special enough to start a dinner party.

# Crème de Céleri aux Noix

## CREAM OF CELERY AND WALNUT SOUP

1 *bunch of celery*
1 *large onion, chopped*
2 tbsp *butter*
1½ quarts *chicken stock*★
*salt and pepper*
½ cup *finely chopped, shelled walnuts*
¾ cup *cream*

Wash and chop the celery, reserving some of the leaves for a garnish. Place the chopped celery and onion in half the butter and cook very gently until the onion is transparent. Add the stock, bring to a boil, season, and simmer for 30 minutes or until the celery is soft. Mill, sieve or liquidize.

Fry the walnuts carefully in the remaining butter over a gentle heat (they burn easily) for a few minutes. Stir into the soup; check seasoning.

To serve, reheat the soup, stir in the cream and garnish with the chopped celery leaves.

The potato was not much used in France before the Revolution; but in Savoy (not then part of France) it was appreciated earlier, and it's from there that the following recipe comes:

# Soupe Montagnarde

## LEEK, POTATO AND CHEESE SOUP
SERVES 6–8

2 *leeks, thinly sliced*
1 *turnip, chopped*
1 *bunch of celery or 1 celeriac, chopped*
1 *large onion, chopped*
¼ cup *butter or diced bacon*
2–3 *large potatoes, peeled and sliced*
1½ quarts *light stock*★
*salt and pepper*
2 cups *milk*
*croûtons or slices of toast*
1 cup *shredded hard cheese*

Briskly brown all the vegetables except the potatoes in the butter or bacon. Turn down the heat, cover, and cook very gently for 10–15 minutes or so. Add the potatoes, stir, then moisten with the stock. Season and simmer for about 40 minutes. Add the milk and simmer for a further 5–10 minutes.

Place the croûtons or toast in the *soupière* (tureen), cover with the cheese and pour the soup over. Serve at once.

Deepest winter threw one onto the resources of the pantry – chiefly dried legumes and home-cured produce, which were often combined in soup.

# Soupe aux Lentilles à la Ménagère

## HOUSEWIFE'S LENTIL SOUP
SERVES 4–5

3 oz *slab bacon, diced*
6 tbsp *butter*
¼ cup each *diced white of leek and carrot*
1 *stalk celery, chopped*
½ cup *dried lentils (red or brown)*
1 *small onion stuck with a clove*
*bay leaf*
*salt, pepper, nutmeg*
1 pair *Strasbourg sausages or approx.*
   ½ lb *fresh sausage*
1 heaping tbsp *flour*

Fry the bacon until the fat runs, add 2 tbsp butter and sweat the chopped vegetables. Put the lentils in a pan with 1½ quarts of cold, unsalted water and bring to a boil; skim if necessary. Add the bacon, vegetables, cloved onion and bay leaf and simmer for 20 minutes or until the lentils are tender but not mushy. Season well with salt, pepper and nutmeg.

Cut the sausages into rounds and brown them in 2 tbsp butter; set aside. In another pan make a roux with the remaining butter and the flour. Cook to a golden brown, then mix in a ladleful of the soup; stir until it boils, then add to rest of the soup. Just before serving, remove the onion and add the browned sausages to the soup.

Some dried legumes, especially chick peas and lima beans, also make super salads. Mix any beans left over from soups with drained, canned tuna, chopped sweet red and green peppers and thinly-sliced raw onion, and then toss in a vinaigrette dressing★ – mint-flavored if liked.

LEFT *Walnuts, celery and cream combine to make delicious Crème de Céleri aux Noix*

16

ABOVE *Leeks and potatoes are enriched with toast and cheese in Soupe Montagnarde; fried sausage adds interest to Soupe aux Lentilles à la Ménagère*

Seaside cooks found time to glean shrimps and rockfish from rock pools at low tide. If there was a fisherman in the family there would always be broken, bony and unsaleable fish to put to good use (see *bouillabaisse*, page 24). Such fishy scraps make wonderful soup but are not normally sold by fish merchants in this country.

# Soupe de Poissons

## BASIC FISH SOUP
### SERVES 4–6

In lieu of rockfish, use a combination of different types of white fish, mackerel, herring and smelts – all cleaned and roughly chopped.

Soften 4–5 chopped garlic cloves and 2 chopped onions in 6 tbsp olive oil. Add 2 lbs *mixed* fish (see above), 8 chopped ripe tomatoes and/or 3 tbsp tomato paste and 2 quarts cold water; bring slowly to a boil. Add a bouquet garni, bay leaf, 2 chopped potatoes and plenty of seasoning; simmer for 30 minutes.

Strain a little at a time, pressing through as much fish flesh as possible. A pinch of powdered saffron (or turmeric) will add flavor and color, and a handful of pasta (optional) gives Mediterranean character. Check the seasoning and reheat (boil for 10 minutes if you are using pasta).

Spread toasted rounds of French bread with *rouille* (see below), float them on the soup and sprinkle everything with shredded cheese for an authentic southern touch.

# Rouille

## SAUCE FOR FISH SOUP

Beat 2 crushed garlic cloves into 2 egg yolks and whisk in 6–7 tbsp olive oil drop by drop, as for mayonnaise★. Add ½ tsp saffron powder (or turmeric) and season with salt and pepper to taste, plus a *little* cayenne or chili powder (optional). (Photograph on p. 25)

For centuries there was a salt tax in France – the infamous *gabelle*, cause of innumerable riots. It was one of the most hated and iniquitous methods of raising money to pay for the usually unnecessary and highly unpopular wars France fought between the fifteenth and seventeenth centuries, and it made salt almost unattainably expensive to the vast majority of the populace, who had to learn other ways of adding savor to their daily fare.

Those lucky enough to make their own wine used it to flavor soup almost as often as they drank it. In some regions they made a virtue of necessity and even produced a *soupe au vin* in which flamed wine was the major ingredient. Wine soup and – in the hop-growing areas of the north and north-east – beer soup may still be found today. By all means try them if you come across them; they are an interesting experience, but I wouldn't go as far as to number them among the delights of French gastronomy.

If you express a genuine interest in traditional cooking among French people who find you *sympathique*, you may be introduced (hesitantly, and probably with some half-embarrassed laughter) to a widespread ancient custom. Variously named *le chabrol, chabrot* or *chabreau* according to district, it consists of pouring a few spoonfuls of wine into the last of your *potage*, mixing briefly and then drinking straight from the bowl.

Some of France's heartiest soups are the *garbures*; *garbure blanche* from Béarn is a very old one – a two-day simmer-up of white beans, white cabbage and potato splendidly flavored with *confits* (see p. 108). The following soup, again fairly substantial, is quite different:

# Garbure aux Laitues ou aux Choux

## LETTUCE OR CABBAGE GARBURE
SERVES 4–6

Carpet a big saucepan with $\frac{1}{2}$lb bacon slices and cover with $\frac{3}{4}$lb chopped veal for stew. Blanch 4–6 heads of lettuce (or 1–2 small heads of cabbage) for 2 minutes (10 for cabbage); drain well, pressing out all water; cool slightly. Cover the meat with 2–3 *each* chopped carrots and onions and 2 cloves; lay the greens on top, cover with stock* and simmer gently for 1 hour (2 for cabbage.)

Lay a bed of crumbled day-old bread in a flameproof tureen or dish. Lift the greens from the saucepan and cut into halves or quarters lengthwise; heap these onto the bread. Sieve the soup, adding more seasoned stock if necessary (leftover meat could be ground to go into a stuffing, perhaps, for *chou farci* (p. 128)); taste and season as necessary. Pour the soup over the greens, sprinkle with more bread crumbs and brown quickly under a very hot broiler.

Probably the best *garbure* we ever ate came from the Pays Basque, once part of the old kingdom of Navarre:

# Garbure Navarraise

## COLORFUL VEGETABLE SOUP
SERVES 4–6

$\frac{1}{2}$ cup *dried red and/or white beans (kidney, navy, marrow)*
*half a ham hock*
2 *leeks, roughly chopped*
2 *carrots, cut in pieces*
*bouquet garni*
1$\frac{1}{2}$ quarts *beef stock*
$\frac{1}{4}$ cup *pork (or goose) fat*
1 *large onion, chopped*
*cayenne, paprika*
3–4 *potatoes, peeled and chopped roughly*
*handful green beans, broken*
*handful shelled fresh fava or lima beans*
*small head cabbage, chopped*
2 *or more pieces of* confit de canard *(p. 109) or several individual* choux farcis *(p. 128)*

Soak the dried beans overnight. Rinse. Put them in a large pan with the ham hock, leeks, carrots and bouquet garni; cover generously with stock. Bring to a boil, skim and simmer for 3 hours, or until the ham starts to fall from the bone. Remove the hock, cut the meat into bite-size pieces and return them to the pot.

Heat the fat in another pan and soften the onions in it, adding a pinch or two of cayenne and paprika. Add to the main pot together with the potatoes, fresh beans and cabbage, adding the *choux farcis* and more stock if necessary (but all *garbures* should be thick enough to stand a spoon in). Simmer for at least 35 minutes longer; taste and season.

If using *confit*, melt the excess fat from it 30 minutes before serving, and add the meat to the pan to warm through and impart its rich flavor. (When serving, try to divide the *confit* so that each diner gets some in his bowl.)

OPPOSITE *Garbure Navarraise*

BELOW *Dried legumes, semolina (for couscous) and a variety of olives on sale in a market*

# Poissons, Crustaces et Fruits de Mer

## FISH AND SEAFOOD

One of the pleasures of eating in France is the positive galaxy of fish and shellfish which appears at tables everywhere – many of them varieties which we rarely if ever see at home, even though they may be just as indigenous here as there. I'm not speaking of the slightly "exotic" species such as fresh anchovies, but of those which are quite commonly found around our shores and in our inland waters.

ABOVE *Red snapper on a bed of salt. Baking fish in salt is a simple and low calorie way of cooking many types of fresh fish. See Daurade au Sel*

We have millions of amateur anglers pulling tons of fish from our rivers and lakes every day for three-quarters of the year. Some of them are sensible enough to make good use of their catch, but usually it is thrown back or cut up for bait after the all-important "weigh-in" at the end of competitions. Similarly, dozens of edible varieties are dumped at sea or at the quayside, exported, or used for industrial purposes.

Because we have forgotten how to cook these useful fish (and there is a sorry inevitability about this), they are no longer offered for sale in the markets. And this lack of demand from retailers means that the fishermen have no incentive to catch or keep them. A sad state of affairs which, one hopes, will improve as we re-learn the value of the still-plentiful protein in the sea.

Our recipes feature species which *are* readily obtainable, though some may call for greater efforts to find than others. With the best will in the world, fish supplies are erratic – affected by season, weather and other variables. Alternatives are often suggested.

Why not bake more fish? It is very simple to prepare, and the fish will usually look after itself, leaving you free to work on vegetables or prepare other courses, or to spend time with your guests.

Take a washed, drawn (and scaled where appropriate) fish and lay it in a greased shallow baking dish. If liked, surround it with chopped onion and/or mashed tomato, and tuck 2 bay leaves or a sprinkle of herbs in the cavity; a thick fish will benefit from three incisions cut in the upper side. Moisten it with a small glass of dry white wine or hard cider, or brush liberally with oil, and bake it for 15–20 minutes per pound at 350°F, according to thickness. This treatment is suitable for many fish, including bass, red snapper, carp and striped mullet.

To improve less tasty fish (pike, hake, perch, whiting and so on), make a stuffing. Sweat in butter or oil *some* of the following: chopped onion, sliced mushrooms, diced ham or bacon, chopped blanched sorrel or spinach, small shelled shrimp, or whatever takes your fancy. Mix in chopped parsley (generously) or herbs (sparingly) and a few bread crumbs, season well and stuff the fish before baking. Remember to allow for stuffing weight when calculating cooking time. Here are some variations:

# Daurade au Sel

## PORGY BAKED IN SALT

Dress a 2¼ lbs porgy or similar fish; leave it whole.

Generously grease a large shallow baking dish and lay the chosen fish in the center. Cover completely, as evenly as possible, with sea salt; you'll need about 4 cups. Bake in a preheated 450°F oven for about 40 minutes.

Serve in the baking dish: push the salt to the sides of the dish, then peel back the skin, trying not to let any salt come into contact with the flesh. Give each diner one fillet (quarter) on a warm plate. Accompany with a wedge of lemon.

# Poisson en Papillotte

### FISH PARCEL

Prepare a fish as for baking (see general text above), with or without stuffing. Butter or oil a large piece of parchment paper or foil; fold it loosely around the fish but make sure it's securely closed. Bake as above – or cook under a hot broiler (use foil in this case!). A good way of retaining the succulent juices.

A pleasantly unexpected way of serving fish is with mustard. Try French *moutarde forte* – medium strength and a pretty yellow color. "Neat" English is rather too strong to use on its own, but may be blended with French – or try one of the fancy varieties now available.

# Maquereaux à la Moutarde

### MACKEREL IN MUSTARD SAUCE
### SERVES 3 AS A MAIN COURSE, 6 AS AN APPETIZER

Draw and wash 3 fresh mackerel (leaving heads on); lay them in a well-buttered baking dish. Stir 3–4 tbsp mustard (see above) into 1 cup *crème fraîche*★ or cream. Add the juice of a lemon, and salt and pepper. Pour this sauce over the fish, garnish with orange and/or lemon slices and dot with butter (about $\frac{1}{4}$ cup). Bake for 25 minutes in a preheated 375°F oven. Serve sprinkled with 2 heaping tbsp chopped parsley (or incorporate this in the sauce before cooking).

The next recipe, from Marseille, is something of a surprise. The one after it is a Norman specialty and is not baked but cooked on top of the range.

# Rougets en Berceau

### RED MULLET IN THEIR CRADLES

2 *eggplants, approx. same length as the fish*
*juice of $\frac{1}{2}$ lemon*
*salt and pepper*
4 *red or striped mullet*
3–4 tbsp *oil*
$1\frac{1}{2}$ lbs *tomatoes*
*pinch saffron ( optional )*
3 tbsp *chopped parsley*

Wipe and halve the eggplants lengthwise, cutting off the stalks. Hollow out the insides, leaving a good ½ inch "wall" at the sides and a slightly thicker base; shave a bit off the base of any that are too rounded to sit level. Brush the insides sparingly with lemon juice, and sprinkle with salt and pepper. Arrange the halves side by side in a baking dish.

Dress, wash and dry the fish, and lay them in their eggplant "cradles". Season with salt and pepper and carefully dribble over two-thirds of the oil. Bake in a preheated 350°F oven for 15 minutes.

Meanwhile skin, seed and roughly chop the tomatoes. Take the dish from the oven and sprinkle the fish with more salt and pepper and saffron. Arrange the tomatoes over and around the "cradles" and moisten them with the remaining oil; scatter the parsley over. Turn the oven up to 400°F to finish cooking – 20–25 minutes according to the size of the fish.

# Filets de Sole Dieppoise

### SOLE, DIEPPE-STYLE

1 pint *fresh mussels*
6 tbsp *butter plus more for greasing dish*
2 *soles* (1 lb each), *filleted, but keep bones, heads and fins*
5 tbsp *dry white wine or hard cider*
*thyme, bay leaf*
1 tbsp *finely chopped parsley*
1 *onion, finely chopped*
¾ cup *sliced mushrooms*
*salt and pepper*
1 cup *shelled small shrimp*
4 *egg yolks*
¼ cup *cream (optional)*

Prepare the mussels★; heat one-third of the butter in a pan and turn the mussels over a brisk heat until they open. Remove the shells and reserve the mussels. Strain the liquid into a large pan. Add to it the fish trimmings, wine, herbs and onion, and 2 cups water, then cover and simmer for 30 minutes. Strain through a cloth.

Heat half the remaining butter and sweat the mushrooms until the juice runs; add this to the strained fish stock (*fumet*), reserving the mushrooms. Reduce the *fumet* by one-third over a medium heat; season to taste.

Wash the fillets and beat them lightly to stop them curling up in cooking; lay them in a buttered flameproof dish with the mussels and shrimp on top. Spoon in just enough *fumet* to cover the sole but not the shellfish (keeping the remaining *fumet* hot); cover and simmer for 10 minutes.

To make the sauce, beat the yolks with the cream; stir the yolk mixture vigorously into the remaining *fumet*, off the heat. Beat in the remaining butter (chilled), bit by bit.

Arrange the sole in a serving dish with the shellfish and mushrooms; spoon the sauce over.

OPPOSITE *Mackerel in Mustard Sauce, ready to go into the oven*
ABOVE *Red Mullet in Eggplant Cradles, covered in a tomato "blankets"*
BELOW *Sole Dieppe-style, garnished with mussels and shrimp in a cream-and-white-wine sauce*

Trout – exquisitely-flavored – are good enough to serve *tout simple*: fry them in butter and remove to a hot serving plate. Add crumbs and parsley, capers or flaked almonds to the pan, fry gently for 1–2 minutes and pour over the fish with the pan juices.

For a summer party this Burgundian recipe, which can be made well in advance, has considerable appeal.

# Truite en Gelée

## TROUT IN WINE JELLY

2 quarts *white wine* court bouillon★
4 *medium-size trout*
slices of tomato, carrot, truffle, lemon,
    *tarragon leaves etc., for decoration*
egg whites *for clarifying* bouillon★
2 *envelopes unflavoured gelatin*
lemon slices, *for garnish*

### For green sauce
1¼ cups *mayonnaise*★
*fresh parsley, chervil, tarragon, chopped
    (proportions to taste, but these must be
    fresh; dried ones will make it taste
    bitter. If only parsley is available, add
    a little lemon juice to give extra
    flavor.)*
1–2 tsp *lemon juice*
*salt*

Make *court bouillon*; simmer to reduce by half.

Draw and wash the trout, removing the backbones if you can do it neatly. Slide them gently into the simmering liquid; poach very gently (the *bouillon* should barely tremble) for 5 minutes. Leave to cool in the *bouillon*.

When cold, lift out the fish, skin the bodies carefully and arrange on a serving dish; decorate as liked.

Clarify the *bouillon*★. Dissolve the gelatin in a little of the clarified *bouillon*, then stir this back into the remainder. Cool slightly and when it starts to thicken, spoon carefully over the decorated trout and leave in a cold place to set.

For the sauce: prepare the mayonnaise and gently but thoroughly stir in the herbs until it's a pretty green color. Add lemon juice and salt to taste. Transfer to a small serving bowl and garnish with lemon slices.

In more pious times than ours, fish was compulsory eating on fast-days – if you could afford it.

Once upon a time (it's said) St Peter, in the guise of an exhausted pilgrim, begged a meal from a poor widow in her little stone hut by the sea. With only scraps in the kitchen, she opened her last bottle of wine for him while awaiting the return of her two fisherman sons. Alas, they'd caught only a few ill-assorted fish and a handful of shellfish; the mother apologetically began to make a dismal fry-up for her guest. But he took over, preparing and cooking the fish with the family's meager stock of oil, herbs, onions, saffron and the last of the wine . . . and invented *bouillabaisse*. This "miracle" complete, he blessed them and vanished in a silvery cloud – presumably leaving them to make their fortune from the new "delicacy."

True *bouillabaisse*, most famous of all fish stews, is made with Mediterranean species. Other popular fish stews in France include *cotriade* from Brittany, *marmite du bord de mer* (Normandy), *pochouse* (Burgundy) and any number of *chaudemers, bouillitures, chaudrées* and *matelotes. Vendredi Saint* (Good Friday) often meant such fish stews. Here is a provençal recipe which uses a mixture of white fish, much simpler than *bouillabaisse*:

BELOW *Trout in Wine Gelatin is a decorative way of serving fish for a dinner party, accompanied by a refreshing herb mayonnaise. It's both pretty and simple to make*

# Aigo-Sau

## FISH STEW

As with all fish stews, it's best to include several different varieties of fish if possible. If you include squid or shellfish, add them later (e.g. squid, scallops, uncooked shrimp about 5 minutes before the end, mussels only a minute or so).

2 lbs *mixed white fish (whiting, cod, halibut, bass etc.)*
2–3 *potatoes, peeled and sliced*
2 *medium-size onions, sliced*
1–2 *tomatoes, skinned and chopped roughly*
*stalk of celery*
2–3 *garlic cloves, crushed*
*salt and pepper*
*bay leaf*
2 tbsp *chopped parsley*
*chopped fennel or dill, to taste*
*strip of orange peel*
3 tbsp *olive oil*
*slices of French bread, warmed*
*chopped parsley and* rouille *(p. 17) to serve*

Cut the fish into convenient-sized boneless chunks and put them in a large heavy pan with the vegetables, garlic, seasoning, herbs and orange peel. Sprinkle the oil over, add 1 quart boiling water and simmer gently for 10–15 minutes or until the fish is cooked.

Bake 1–2 slices of bread per person until crisp but not brown.

Stir the *aigo-sau* gently, then serve in individual warmed bowls and sprinkle the parsley over. Hand the hot crisp bread and *rouille* separately.

ABOVE *Aigo-Sau is a Provençal fish stew. For best results use a mixture of different white fish and shellfish*

A cheap and easy "Good Friday" dish is this one from Roussillon. For *Congre aux Raisins Secs* (eel with raisins), soak 1 cup raisins in white wine or dry hard cider until plump. Dust 2 lbs eel chunks in seasoned flour and fry them for 2 minutes in ¼ cup hot oil. Stir in 4 crushed garlic cloves, 2 tbsp chopped parsley and a bouquet garni. Pour in 1 cup tomato sauce*; season, cover and simmer gently for 20 minutes. Add the raisins and their liquid and cook for 15–20 minutes longer on very low heat.

Serve in a shallow bowl surrounded by pieces of bread, fried in oil then rubbed with cut garlic.

"Slippery as an eel" is no myth – but eels are economical and easy to cook, and well worth experimenting with. If your supplier doesn't skin them for you, make eels easier to handle by washing them first in water, then in vinegar. Rinse again if you're *not* going to remove the skin.

If your family are French fries-with-everything fiends, dredge skinned pieces of eel (see above) in seasoned flour. Deep fry, in batches, in hot but not smoking oil until the outsides are crisp and golden – 5–8 minutes according to thickness. Serve with fries – of course!

For *Anguilles Sautées Provençales* (fried eels Provence-style), shallow-fry the pieces in oil and add a sprinkling of chopped garlic and parsley for the final minute of cooking. Either way, serve with lemon wedges.

25

# Anguilles au Vert

## "EELS IN THE GREEN"
SERVES 6

2 *onions, chopped*
¼ cup *butter*
4½ lbs *medium-size eels, skinned and cut into convenient size pieces*
1 *bottle dry white wine, hard cider or wine-and-water*
½ lb *sorrel or spinach, finely chopped*
½ lb *watercress*
*pinch each chopped sage, mint, chervil and savory or thyme*
1 heaping tbsp *chopped parsley*
*salt and pepper*
6 *egg yolks*
1 cup *heavy cream*
*lemon juice (see recipe)*

Soften the onions gently in the butter; raise the heat slightly and add the eel pieces, turning them in the pan to stiffen. Pour on the chosen liquid; add the finely-chopped sorrel or spinach, watercress, herbs and seasoning. Cover, bring to a boil and simmer for 10 minutes.

Beat the egg yolks with the cream and add a few drops of lemon juice (2 or more tsp if you are using spinach instead of sorrel). Take the pan off the heat and thoroughly stir in the yolk mixture to thicken the sauce. Reheat but *do not boil*. Serve hot with croûtes – or cold with boiled or baked potatoes.

Cod is not indigenous to the Mediterranean, yet dried salt cod is madly popular with Provençals – who transform this oddity into myriad delicious dishes. Why? Early Norse seamen wanted to buy oil and wine here – and had only their *stokkfisch* to barter with. It has long been a "provençal" delicacy: a *santon* (one of the carved wooden figures placed around Christmas crèches since time immemorial) shows *morue* being offered to the infant Jesus. Raïto sauce, in the following recipe, is even older – having arrived with the first Greek colonizers. How, I wonder, did the two get together? The *gros souper*, a lengthy meal eaten after Midnight Mass on Christmas Eve, often features dried cod.

# Morue en Rayte

## SALT COD WITH WINE, CAPERS AND OLIVES
SERVES 4–6

2 lbs *dried salt cod*
1 *large onion, finely chopped*
2 tbsp *olive oil plus oil for frying*
¼ cup *flour*
2 cups *fish or chicken stock★*
2 cups *red wine*
2–4 *garlic cloves, crushed*
3 tbsp *tomato paste*
1 tbsp *fennel or dill seeds (optional)*
*bouquet garni*
*black pepper*
2 tbsp *capers*
2 tbsp *ripe olives, pitted*

Soak the cod in cold water for *at least* 24 hours, changing the water often.

Soften the onion in 2 tbsp oil, stir in 1 tbsp flour and add the stock and wine. Bring to a boil, adding the garlic, tomato paste, fennel or dill seeds, bouquet garni and a good seasoning of pepper. Simmer to thicken and reduce by half.

Meanwhile trim the cod carefully and cut it into chunks. Dry it on paper towels, coat it in the rest of the flour and brown it briskly in hot oil for 3 minutes. Put the cod into the sauce, together with the capers and olives; cook together for about 10 minutes. Serve in a hot dish surrounded with triangles of fried bread.

LEFT *Top: Anguilles au Vert (eels with a creamy but piquant green sauce). Below: Morue en Rayte (dried salt cod in a red wine sauce with capers and olives)*

Brittany is famous for seafood. Their simple, delicious way with mollusks is to open them, add a little "snail butter" (see below) to the fishy half, sprinkle them with crumbs and cook under a scorching broiler for 1–5 minutes according to size. The photograph above shows *pétoncles* (a type of mini-scallop), but the same treatment will do for clams, mussels – even scallops and oysters, if you don't think it a waste!

To make Snail Butter for a quart of large shellfish (you need rather more for smaller shellfish): slightly soften $\frac{1}{2}$ cup butter and work in 2 tbsp each minced onion and chopped parsley, 2 crushed garlic cloves, salt, pepper and cayenne to taste.

If you're feeling expansive, a few drops of brandy sprinkled over just before broiling won't go amiss. Or here's a more sophisticated mixture:

ABOVE *Pétoncles (mini-scallops), broiled with "snail butter," recipe left*

*Beurre Breton*: marinate 2 shallots, 2 tbsp parsley and 3 garlic cloves (all finely chopped), 2 pinches each pepper and apple pie spice in 3–4 tbsp dry white wine for an hour or two before working into $\frac{1}{2}$ cup softened butter.

27

"Around the corner" from Brittany are Poitou and Vendée. Over the ages a vast bay silted up to make a 175,000-acre marsh. Between the eleventh and seventeenth centuries it was drained, partly by Dutch engineers, and transformed into a fascinating area of lush pasture called the *marais poitevin*. Thousands of narrow canals wind about among tiny fields, whose grazing can often be reached only by cattle-carrying punts. Trees arch over the water to create a maze of cool, green tunnels, through which you can make lovely peaceful boat trips.

The coast is ideal for mussels, used to make many varieties of *mouclade* – a local specialty. Here's one version.

For 2 servings, prepare 2 quarts fresh mussels★. Put them in a big pan with 1 cup *each* dry white wine and heavy cream, 2 heaping tbsp minced onion and a little salt. Bring to a boil and shake over the heat for about 5–6 minutes to make the mussels open. Strain the liquid into another pan, add 2 heaping tbsp chopped parsley and 1 tsp curry powder; leave to reduce and thicken over a medium heat.

Discard the empty half-shells and arrange the mussels in shallow serving bowl(s); pour the sauce over the mussels.

BELOW *A glimpse of the marais poitevin*
OPPOSITE *Mussels in Ham Sauce*

Further south, the treatment of mussels is heartier. *Abitarela* is the *langue d'Oc* word for the sort of small country inn which has provided a clean bed and a simple but tasty meal for travelers since the Middle Ages.

# Moules à l'Abitarela

### MUSSELS WITH HAM SAUCE

The original recipe given to us seemed awfully complicated. We found that the same ingredients, with this simplified method, were just as good.

1–2 *onions, finely chopped*
2 *cloves*
*bouquet garni*
*sprig of rosemary (or thyme)*
3–5 *garlic cloves*
2 cups *dry white wine*
¾ cup *diced cooked ham*
1 *shallot, chopped*
3–4 tbsp *oil*
1 tbsp *flour*
2–3 tbsp *tomato paste*
4 quarts *fresh mussels*
*salt and pepper*
*saffron (optional)*
*paprika (optional)*

Cook the onions, cloves, bouquet garni, herbs and 2–4 garlic cloves (chopped) in half the wine until very soft. Discard the cloves, bouquet garni and herb stalks; mill or liquidize.

Meanwhile, brown the ham and shallot in the oil; stir in the remaining garlic (crushed), the flour and tomato paste, then moisten with the cooked purée.

Prepare the mussels★ and cook them in the remaining wine over a brisk heat, shaking the pan until they are all open. Strain the liquid through a fine cloth into the sauce; reheat, taste and season with salt (if required), pepper, saffron and paprika. Add more liquid if necessary to make a thick pouring consistency.

Discard the empty mussel shells, arrange the full halves in heated shallow bowls and spoon the sauce over.

Scallops are marvelous shellfish – rich, tasty and decorative. Try these two contrasting recipes.

# Coquilles aux Poireaux

## BAKED SCALLOPS WITH LEEKS
### SERVES 6

6 *large (or* 9 *small) leeks or* 1 *bunch scallions*
1 lb *scallops (thawed if frozen)*
*butter (see recipe)*
*salt, pepper, cayenne*
1¼ cups *heavy cream or* crème frâiche★
*nutmeg*
*grated Parmesan cheese (optional)*

Cut off the green parts of the leeks (reserve for soup). Wash and trim the white parts, tie them loosely in bundles and cook them in boiling salted water for 5–6 minutes. Refresh them in cold water and drain very thoroughly, pressing out all water. If using scallions, trim them, retaining the pale green section of stalk and cutting off any bulbs that are swollen. Blanch in salted water for 2 minutes, then drain thoroughly. Cut into ½ inch sections.

Butter 6 small ovenproof serving dishes or scallop shells (or one large dish), and put in the leeks or scallions, then the scallops. Season with salt, freshly-ground pepper and a pinch of cayenne. Cover completely with cream and sprinkle over the nutmeg and Parmesan (if liked). Bake in a preheated 400°F oven for 10–15 minutes.

# Brochette de Coquilles St Jacques

## SKEWERED SCALLOPS

Thaw 20 scallops (if necessary) and thread them on four kabob skewers, alternating with small tomato halves and little of slab bacon. Brush with melted butter or oil.

Cook under the broiler, about 5 inches away from the heat, for 4–5 minutes each side, basting often. Sprinkle with finely chopped fresh herbs (fennel, dill, tarragon) and serve with tomato sauce★ spiked with a pinch of cayenne or a few drops of hot pepper sauce. To make a main course, accompany with plain rice and salad.

OPPOSITE *Oysters in a Breton Market*          BELOW *Baked Scallops with Leeks (top) with Skewered Scallops*

# Paëlla Basquais

SERVES 8–10

2 quarts *fresh mussels*
2 quarts *fresh clams*
*dry white wine (optional)*
3½ lbs *small chicken pieces*
4–5 tbsp *cooking oil*
1 *large onion, chopped*
1 *large sweet red pepper, diced*
1 *large green pepper, diced*
½ lb *chorizo or other spiced sausage,*
    *thickly sliced*
½ lb *raw ham (e.g. Bayonne) or ordinary*
    *cooked ham, diced*
4 *large garlic cloves, chopped*
¾ lb *hake, cut into chunks*
2⅓ cups *long-grain rice*
*salt, pepper*
½–1 tsp *saffron (or 1 tsp turmeric)*
2½ cups *chicken stock★*
*chopped parsley, to decorate*
8–10 *whole jumbo shrimp or crayfish for*
    *garnish (optional)*

Scrub the shellfish and put them in a
pan with 2½ cups water or water/wine
mixed. Bring to a boil quickly and cook
fast for 5 minutes to open them. Drain,
reserving the liquid, and remove from
their shells.

Brown the chicken pieces in the hot
oil in a large thick-bottomed saucepan;
add the onion and diced peppers. Turn
down the heat and cook for 6–7
minutes; stir in the sausage, ham, garlic
and hake. The ingredients should be
well coated with oil at this stage; if
necessary, add a little more.

Add the rice and stir-fry for
2 minutes, then add the saffron (or
turmeric), pepper and a little salt. Mix
the stock with the reserved shellfish
liquid and add water if necessary to
make up to 5 cups. Add to the pan, just
covering the ingredients; cover and
simmer gently for 15–20 minutes or
until the liquid is absorbed.

If using shrimp or crayfish for the
garnish, cook them in fast-boiling
water for 10–12 minutes (no longer) or
until they are bright red.

Mix the mussels and clams into the
paëlla. Heat through, sprinkle with
chopped parsley, and decorate with the
jumbo shrimp or crayfish.

ABOVE *Paëlla Basquais reflects the Spanish influence in the Basque region of France. In this area they love to serve broiled crustacea – especially crayfish – hot with cold sauces: Mayonnaise★, Aïoli★, Sauce Romesco★.*

*On the Catalan coast, they fry (rather than boil) shrimp in a little hot oil with lots of freshly ground black pepper*

BELOW *A miscellany of fish for bouillabaisse*

*Calamars, calmars* and *encornets* all mean squid and are popular around French coasts. Whether fresh or frozen, squid is available coast to coast and is one of the most inexpensive shellfish available.

# Calmars Farcis

## STUFFED SQUID
### (CHOICE OF STUFFINGS)

### Catalan Stuffing from Roussillon
1 cup *chopped almonds*
1 *onion, chopped*
4–5 *garlic cloves, crushed*
2 heaping tbsp *chopped parsley*
¾ cup *diced cooked ham*
large slice *fried bread, crumbled*
salt, pepper, pinch cayenne
1 *egg*

Mix all the ingredients together with the chopped tentacles of the squid (see below), and bind with the egg.

### Provençal stuffing from Marseille
10 oz *bulk spinach*
large *fillet of whiting or other cheap fish*
*salt and pepper, oil*

Cook the spinach in a very little boiling salted water for 2–3 minutes; drain and squeeze out *all* water, then chop finely. Blanch the fish in boiling water for 5 minutes or until flesh flakes easily; drain and trim off any bones or skin. Mix with spinach, seasoning and chopped tentacles (see below), then cook in a little very hot oil for 5 minutes.

### The Squid
4 *medium-size squid*
2 tbsp *seasoned flour*
½ cup *oil*
1 *onion, chopped*
½ cup *dry white wine*
1 cup *tomato sauce★*
*chicken stock★ (optional)*
*bouquet garni*
*pinch saffron*
*salt and pepper*

Prepare the squid★ and leave covered in cold water.

Chop the *best* bits of heads and tentacles and add them to whichever stuffing you have chosen. Drain and dry the squid, stuff with chosen *farce* and sew up the ends. Dredge with seasoned flour.

In a pan large enough to take the squid in a single layer, heat the oil and brown the squid on all sides; lift out carefully. Soften the onion in the same oil without coloring it. When the onion is transparent, stir in the remaining flour to make a white roux; moisten with the wine and tomato sauce, bring to a boil and add sufficient water or chicken stock to make enough sauce just to cover the squid. Add the bouquet, saffron and seasoning.

Bring back to a boil, replace the squid carefully, cover and simmer as gently as possible for 30–40 minutes.

Serve on a heated dish with the sauce poured around, accompanied by plain boiled rice.

BELOW *Stuffed Squid in Tomato Sauce. The ends have been left unsewn to show the two different types of stuffing*

# Volailles et Gibiers à Plume

## POULTRY AND FEATHERED GAME

Most French country people still keep poultry: hens; ducks and geese when they have space and water; guinea-fowl ("*so* much easier to rear than turkeys") – and sometimes quail. If they don't have their own, they buy them live at the local weekly markets along with the townsfolk. So the domestic birds on French tables are almost always "fresh" – to the benefit of diners.

Everyone, of course, sometimes eats tired old stewing chicken, especially in mountain areas like Savoy, where chickens are reared for eggs, not eating. We loved one great-grandfather's "recipe" (Aravis is a local mountain range).

"Take an Aravis hen," he said, "and place it in a pot of salted water with a turnip, a carrot and an onion [standard so far; he had obviously watched his wife in the kitchen] – and a large pebble." At this point the old man began to chortle, so the rest of the story came in uneven bursts.

"Leave it to cook steadily," he continued, "at a good simmer, *longtemps, longtemps, longtemps* [for a long, long, long time]." And now he slapped his thigh delightedly, cackling with glee: "You'll know it's done when a fork passes easily into the pebble!"

But years of experience have endowed every region with a number of really terrific ways of transforming these tired old birds into feast-worthy dishes. Our ubiquitous dressed and drawn freezer chickens may also be improved by these flavorsome techniques. (Reduce cooking times by at least a third if you use young birds.)

Henri IV, the colorful French king from Navarre, was credited with saying, "I'm determined that every worker in my kingdom should have a chicken in the pot each Sunday." The classic *poule au pot* recipe from his native far southwest has a stuffing much like the one opposite, with the additions of Bayonne ham and Armagnac brandy. The bird is simmered in a *bouillon* containing lots of onions, carrots, leek, turnip and celery – and not roasted. This is a single meal: the strained *bouillon* makes a delicious soup when poured over chunks of bread, leaving the chicken and vegetables as a second course to eat with potatoes.

LEFT *Hen basking on a Pyrenean windowsill* OPPOSITE *Stuffed Stewing Chicken, a version of Henry IV's famous Poule au Pot. Extra stuffing is rolled in a cloth and boiled alongside the bird*

# Poule Farcie Paysanne

## BOILED STUFFED CHICKEN
SERVES 4–5

1 *stewing chicken approx. 4 lbs*
*fat for greasing*
*wine (optional)*

### For the farce
*gizzard, heart and liver of bird*
$\frac{1}{2}$ lb *cooked ham or raw ham (e.g.*
*Parma)*
$\frac{1}{2}$ lb *fresh pork sides*
$\frac{1}{4}$ lb *lean veal*
$\frac{1}{4}$ lb *slab bacon*
1 *onion*
3 *garlic cloves*
*small handful each parsley and celery*
*leaves*

*larger handful chard leaves, spinach or*
*other greens*
3 slices *crustless bread soaked in a little*
*hot milk*

Grind or process all the above fairly coarsely, then measure. For each 2 cups add:

$\frac{1}{2}$ tsp *salt*
$\frac{1}{4}$ tsp *pepper*
1 *egg*

Mix well. Stuff and sew up the prepared bird. Put the trimmings (neck and so on) into a very large pan with:

4–5 *garlic cloves*
1 *large onion studded with 2 cloves*
*salt and pepper*
*bouquet garni*

Cover generously with cold water and bring to a boil. Add the bird (making sure it is covered), bring back to a boil and simmer very gently for $1\frac{1}{2}$ hours (less for a younger bird).

Meanwhile, shape the remaining *farce* into a sausage and roll up neatly in a fine cloth. Tie the ends securely and cook alongside the bird.

When the bird is cooked, take it out carefully, draining well. Put it in a roasting pan with a little fat underneath and some smeared over the breast. Roast in a preheated 400°F oven – for 20–25 minutes, or until browned to your liking. Remove. Pour off fat and *déglacer* the pan with a little of the stock, to make a gravy (stir in a little wine to taste, if liked).

To serve, give each diner a portion of the bird and some of the stuffing from the interior, plus a slice of the boiled *farce*. (Strained and skimmed of all fat, the cooking liquid makes magnificent stock for future use.)

# Poulet Ste Ménéhould

### CHICKEN WITH BREAD CRUMBS

Simmer the bird in well-flavored chicken stock★ until cooked (juice from a needle-prick in the thigh should be barely colored); drain and pat dry. Paint all over with beaten egg and coat thoroughly with soft bread crumbs. Very carefully drip a little oil or melted butter all over and brown on a spit or under the broiler, or put in a hot oven for 10 minutes, basting carefully.

The following is a simple and intriguing dish, equally suitable for stewing chicken or younger chickens. Don't be alarmed by the quantity of garlic, which is remarkably unpungent when cooked in its skin.

# Poulet Quarante Gousses d'Ail

### BRAISED CHICKEN WITH GARLIC
SERVES 4–5

Sprinkle the inside of a large roaster or stewing chicken with salt and insert 2–3 bay leaves and 2 sprigs of fresh thyme or 1 tsp dried. Put the bird in a large casserole and surround it with 40 *unpeeled* garlic cloves. Dribble $\frac{1}{4}$ cup oil over the bird (or smear with butter), cover tightly and cook in a preheated 350°F oven for $1\frac{1}{2}$–2 hours or until cooked. If preferred, uncover the bird for the last half hour to allow it to brown.

Toast 1–2 slices of bread per diner. Squeeze the garlic flesh from the skins with a fork, mash it and spread on the toast. Serve with the chicken.

ABOVE *Chicken braised with 40 unpeeled garlic cloves has a surprisingly unpungent flavor*

Here is a tasty way with chicken pieces, even frozen ones:

# Poulet Niçoise

## CHICKEN WITH OLIVES

4 *chicken pieces*
8–10 *tiny whole onions, scallions or*
    *shallots*
3 tbsp *olive oil*
2 *onions, sliced*
1 *green pepper, diced*
3–4 *large garlic cloves, crushed*
1 lb *tomatoes, skinned and chopped*
    *roughly*
1 heaping tsp *dried basil, or* ½ tsp
    *oregano and* ½ tsp *savory*
*pinch saffron (optional)*
2 tbsp *tomato paste*
¾ cup *red wine or chicken stock★*
*salt and pepper*
15–20 *pitted ripe olives*
2–4 *anchovy fillets, very finely sliced*
    *(optional)*

Skin the chicken pieces and brown them quickly with the whole onions in very hot oil in a flameproof casserole or stewpan. Remove the chicken and add the sliced onions, green pepper and garlic to the pan; soften over a lowered heat for 5 minutes. Return the chicken to the pan, add the tomatoes, herbs, saffron, tomato paste and wine or stock. Taste, season and cover.

Cook gently until done: about 55 minutes in a preheated 350°F oven or on top of the range for 40–45 minutes.

Halfway through cooking turn the chicken pieces and stir the pan contents. The chicken should be lightly sauced, not in a stew. If the sauce is very thin, cook uncovered for the rest of the cooking time. Add the olives and anchovy fillets about 10 minutes before completion. Check seasoning and serve with rice and a tossed green salad.

OPPOSITE *Bunches of garlic on sale at the Sunday morning market in Amboise*
RIGHT *Garlic, tomatoes, peppers, olives, and of course olive oil, give Poulet Niçoise a splendidly Provençal flavor*

Ducks have such a superb flavor that there are few better ways to serve them than simply roasted. (A rotary spit will give you a succulent bird with a marvelously crisp skin.) Stuffing makes them even more interesting. In southwest France, prunes make their expected appearance (you might substitute dried apricots, perhaps) and feature in an unusual garnish, too (see below and on the cover). Around Marseille, they favor a forcemeat of ground veal, ham and olives – and sometimes even a few grains from the locally-grown lavender heads. The recipe opposite is an adaptation of a favorite Norman dish which is popular all over France though little known over here. Our method obviates the need for a duck press.

# Canard Villeneuvois

## DUCK WITH PRUNES

1 lb (*about 2½ cups*) *prunes*
*red wine or tea for marinating*
*(optional)*
2 *onions, sliced*
2 *carrots, sliced*
*thyme, bay leaf*
3 tbsp *oil*
1 *duckling*
1½ cups *red wine or wine-and-poultry stock*
*salt and pepper*
2 tbsp *Armagnac or brandy (optional)*
*fried bread*

Soak the prunes in red wine, tea or water as necessary; simmer them for 5 minutes in their marinade or in salted water. Soften the vegetables and herbs in the oil for 10 minutes. Pound the duck liver and add it to the pan with the wine; season and simmer gently for 20 minutes. Remove the bay leaf and sieve, mill or liquidize. Add the brandy and the drained prunes; simmer until the prunes are tender.

Place about half the prunes in the duck; prick the duck skin all over and roast in your usual way.

Reheat the remaining prunes and sauce (add the prune liquid or more wine or stock if necessary). Serve the bird surrounded by rounds of fried bread with prunes balanced on them – all very hot.

OPPOSITE *Duck with Prunes*   ABOVE *Rouen-style Duck*

# Canard à la Rouennaise

## DUCK ROUEN-STYLE

1 *large duck (ideally fresh and un-bled)*
½ cup *butter*
*salt and pepper*
1½ cups *red wine*
6 *shallots (or 2 medium-sized onions),*
   *chopped finely*
*beaten egg (for coating)*
*soft bread crumbs*

Smear the duck with two-thirds of the butter, sprinkle with salt and pepper and roast in a preheated 425°F oven for 30–35 minutes (it will be slightly underdone). Meanwhile finely crush the duck liver (and any other poultry liver you may have) and cover with 2 tbsp of the wine. Brown the shallots in the remaining butter and then moisten with the rest of the wine. Leave to simmer and reduce by about a third. Take off the heat and stir in the liver mixture; keep warm.

Take the duck from the oven and carve it into serving pieces (2 breasts, 2 legs, 2 wings), making sure to catch the juices. Break up the carcass, from which more juices will run, and add these to the sauce. Strain the sauce and correct the seasoning.

Slice the breasts, arrange them on an ovenproof serving dish and spoon the sauce over. Cover and put in a much cooler oven (350°F), where they will cook a little more while you finish the rest. Meanwhile paint the leg and wing joints with beaten egg and coat with bread crumbs. Broil or fry them to brown the surfaces and complete their cooking. Serve the sauced breasts and crumbed pieces separately. Accompany with plain potatoes.

Wood, or wild, pigeon is a bird which is less popular in France than it was. The Basques have an elaborate netting routine for catching a proportion of the wood pigeons that migrate over their region each autumn.

We can adapt the methods for cooking wood pigeon to our own domesticated young pigeons, or squabs, specially bred for the table.

Pigeons are relatively inexpensive to buy and make a welcome change from chicken, although they may be cooked by almost as many methods. Young ones (squab) would be super cooked in the same way as the Norman Partridge on p. 45 – using almost any fruit. But the simplest method of all, suitable for birds of any age, is to roast them. Serve accompanied with liver-flavored croûtes.

# Palombes Rôties

## ROAST PIGEON
SERVES 3

3 *slices bacon*
3 *pigeons*
¼ cup *pork or goose fat, softened*
*salt and pepper*
2–3 *chicken livers (unless the pigeons have their own livers)*
*butter for frying*
¼ cup *Armagnac (or other brandy) or sherry*
3 (or 6) *slices bread*

Wrap the bacon slices around the pigeons, then smear the birds all over with the softened fat. Sprinkle with salt and pepper and roast in a preheated 450°F oven on a rack above a roasting pan – or on a spit. Allow 15–25 minutes for young birds; if their age is suspect, cook at 375°F for correspondingly longer, basting often.

Fry the livers briefly and mash to a creamy paste with a few drops of the spirit or wine. Fry the bread until crisp and golden; spread with the paste and keep warm.

Remove the bacon from the birds and place them on the croûtes; *déglacer* the roasting pan (or tray below the spit) with the remaining brandy or wine to make a sauce. Hand this separately.

Roast pigeons are traditionally served with fresh green peas and bacon bits.

If liked, the pigeons can be stuffed with the following *farce*: chop the livers and tender parts of the gizzards with 3–4 slices bacon and ½ cup bulk sausage-meat. Add a crushed garlic clove, 2 tbsp chopped parsley, salt and pepper. Bind with an egg.

Or here's another stuffing, originally created for wild duck (*Sarcelle au Citron*), but good for all dark-meat game birds. Work the finely chopped rind of a lemon into ¼ cup butter with the chopped bird's liver, salt, pepper and the juice of a lemon. Put this mixture in the body cavity. Lay 2 slices of lemon (more for bigger birds) on the breast and secure under a slice of bacon. Roast in the oven or on a spit. Make a gravy from the pan juices and chicken stock.

OPPOSITE *Spit-roasting makes for succulent birds. On the spit are wood-pigeon (left) and teal (wild duck) with lemon stuffing*
BELOW *Périgord geese, traditionally raised for foie gras, hurrying to the river for a bath*

# Salmis de Palombes

## PIGEON RAGOÛT
SERVES 4–5

5–6 oz *Canadian bacon, diced*
1 tbsp *oil*
1 *onion, chopped*
1½ cups *sliced mushrooms*
2 *carrots, sliced*
1 *garlic clove, crushed*
2 tbsp *tomato paste*
1 tbsp *flour*
1 quart *red wine and chicken stock*★
 *(proportions as convenient)*
*bouquet garni*
1 *chopped truffle (optional)*
1–2 *pinches apple pie spice*
*salt and pepper*
*pinch cayenne*
3–4 *pigeons*
6 tbsp *butter*
at least ¼ cup *Armagnac or other brandy (or full-bodied red wine)*

Gently fry the bacon in the oil, then add the onion, mushrooms, carrots and garlic; stir with a spatula and, when starting to brown, incorporate the tomato paste. Sprinkle in the flour, stir until colored slightly, then moisten with the wine and stock. Add the bouquet, truffle, spice and seasonings. Cover and simmer for 30 minutes.

Meanwhile, cook the pigeons in the butter in a covered stewpan, turning often to brown evenly all over. After 20 minutes take them out, and remove the leg portions and breasts from the carcasses (they will still be fairly bloody). Break up the carcasses and put them, along with any trimmings, giblets and juices, into the sauce; simmer for another 15 minutes. Put the serving pieces into a shallow, flameproof dish, pour the brandy over and *flamber*; extinguish by covering with a lid. Remove the dish to a warm place.

Sieve the sauce, pressing through as much as possible. To serve, reheat the sauce and pour it over the meat. Serve with mashed or steamed potatoes.

Even an ordinary goose is a very rich bird; roasting is a good way of cooking out a lot of the fat, and fruit (apples, dried apricots, prunes) make an excellent accompaniment or stuffing.

This old recipe shows another, more unexpected, way to counteract the richness. It may be adapted for duck.

# Oie à la Moutarde

## GOOSE WITH MUSTARD
SERVES 3–6

Chop the goose liver with shallots, bay leaf, parsley, chives, thyme and basil (or as large a selection of fresh herbs as available); season, and use as part of your stuffing. Stuff the prepared goose, prick the skin all over with a fork and roast the bird on a rack in a roasting pan in a 350°F oven for 44 minutes per kilo/20 minutes per pound – or in your usual way. Spoon off the fat in the pan from time to time during cooking.

Fifteen minutes before completion, transfer 2 tbsp fat from the pan to a saucepan and set aside; pour off all remaining fat. Stir 1 heaping tbsp Dijon-style mustard into the pan juices and smear or baste the goose thoroughly; sprinkle with soft bread crumbs and return to finish cooking. Turn up the heat to help brown it.

Stir 1 heaping tbsp flour into the reserved fat to make a roux. Cook slightly to brown, then add 1–2 tbsp lemon juice, 1–2 tbsp Dijon-style mustard and 1 cup skimmed chicken stock*. Hand this sauce separately.

In the southwest and in Alsace, where geese are raised for *foie gras*, goose fat almost takes the place of butter or oil in cooking. Because these fattened birds are expensive, they tend to be used for costly dishes like *confit d'oie* (p. 109), though the Alsatians sometimes cook their geese as part of a Christmas *choucroute*.

Christmas eating in France varies from area to area. In some places the main celebration is on Christmas Eve; big parties share a gargantuan meal, either in a local restaurant or at home. For obvious reasons this is followed by a quiet and simple family day at home. Elsewhere, notably in Provence, Christmas Eve is an abstemious day, but Midnight Mass is followed by the *gros souper*, a mammoth feast lasting most of the night. It might include among other things braised celery, *anchoïade* (p. 123), snails with *aïoli*★, a fish dish, a separate vegetable course and the traditional "thirteen desserts" – though one rarely finds that many served today.

As in the U.S. many French families serve roast turkey for Christmas dinner. It's commonly stuffed with whole cooked chestnuts mixed with ground meats and the brandy-steeped liver.

BELOW *Crumbed Goose with Mustard Sauce*
OPPOSITE *Typical peaceful farm scene*

Fruit has often been cooked with birds in France, especially with game birds or dark-fleshed ones such as ducks. When fresh fruit was not available, grand'mère made use of canned or dried fruit. Prunes and raisins appear with almost anything.

# Faisan aux Raisins

### PHEASANT WITH GRAPES
SERVES 3–4

1 *pheasant, ideally a hen*
*salt and pepper*
4–5 *slices bacon*
½ cup *fat (preferably goose)*
2 lbs *large green grapes*
1 *shallot or small onion, chopped*
¾ cup *red wine*
3–4 tbsp *Armagnac or brandy (optional)*
½ cup *heavy cream or* crème fraîche*
2 tsp *sugar*
*a few drops of lemon juice*
*fried bread to serve*

Season the interior of the bird. Wrap the bacon slices around the bird. Melt half the fat in a large stewpan or casserole and brown the bird all over. Cover and reduce the heat (or place in a 350°F oven), and cook very gently for 30–40 minutes: the bird should be slightly undercooked.

Meanwhile plunge the grapes into boiling water, drain and peel (seed if you're conscientious). Put in a pan with the remaining fat and shallot or onion; stir for a moment or two, then add half the wine. Cook gently for 10 minutes.

Set the pheasant on one side to keep warm and *déglacer* its pan with the rest of the wine and the brandy (alternatively use a little more wine); increase the heat and reduce briskly. Lower heat, stir in the cream and reduce again more gently.

Add grapes and their juice to the sauce. Stir well; add salt, pepper, sugar and a few drops of lemon juice; taste again and adjust seasoning.

Carve the bird into serving portions and place on pieces of fried bread in a shallow serving bowl; stir any juices from the bird into the grape sauce, and spoon on top.

ABOVE *Partridge, Normandy-style.*   BELOW *Pheasant with Grapes*

In Normandy, local recipes favor apples, Calvados and cream.

# Perdreaux à la Normande

## NORMAN PARTRIDGE

Wrap 4 partridges in slices of bacon. Melt 2 tbsp butter and brown them all over, one at a time but in a pan large enough to take them all. Arrange in a single layer in the pan; scatter with thyme (fresh if available), salt and pepper.

Peel and core 4 tart apples and slice into rings; fry for 5 minutes in at least 2 tbsp butter and add to the birds. Cover and simmer *very* gently for 25–30 minutes.

Remove the birds and keep warm. Pour 1 tbsp Calvados into the pan and *flamber*; extinguish with ½ cup cream and stir to mix well. Pour this mixture into a dish and serve the birds on top. Accompany with plainly cooked green vegetables and, if liked, more fried apple rings.

The rather underrated red cabbage makes a fine foil for game, and the cooking method of this next recipe means that the meat will be succulent even if your bird is past its prime.

# Faisan Braisé au Chou Rouge et aux Châtaignes

## PHEASANT WITH RED CABBAGE AND CHESTNUTS

¼ cup *drippings, pork or goose fat*
1 *pheasant*
1 *head red cabbage, shredded (about* 1 lb*)*
2 *onions, sliced*
14 oz *peeled chestnuts*
¾ cup *red wine*
2 tbsp *white wine (or cider) vinegar*
¾ cup *chicken stock*★
*bouquet garni*
*sprig of rosemary (optional)*
*salt and pepper*
*crisp green apple for garnish*

ABOVE *Braised Pheasant with Red Cabbage and fresh chestnuts*

Melt the fat in a flameproof casserole large enough to take the bird and other ingredients comfortably; brown the pheasant briskly all over, then remove to another dish. Add the cabbage and onions to the pan; stir over a medium heat for a few minutes until well coated with fat.

Add the chestnuts, wine, vinegar, stock, herbs and seasoning; nest the bird back in. Bring to a boil and cover tightly. Cook in a preheated 325°F oven for 40–50 minutes, or until pheasant is cooked.

Serve whole or cut up on the vegetables surrounded by slices of the unpeeled apple (dip the slices in lemon-and-water to prevent them turning brown).

This recipe is suitable for partridge too: double the number of birds, wrap them in slices of bacon and reduce the cooking time by a third. Pre-cook the chestnuts for 5–10 minutes.

45

Ever since chocolate came to Europe from Mexico in the sixteenth century, it's been used discreetly to add a subtle overtaste to the gamey flavor of dark-fleshed birds. Use it sparingly for chicken, too – it should not be identifiable by those who aren't in the know!

# Pintadeau au Chocolat

## GUINEA FOWL IN CHOCOLATE SAUCE

1 *young guinea fowl* (2½–3 lbs)
*seasoned flour*
¼ cup *cooking fat (or half fat, half oil)*
1 *medium-size onion, grated*
2 *carrots, diced*
½ tsp *cinnamon*
1 *square (1 oz) unsweetened or cooking chocolate*
*salt and pepper*

Skin and cut up the fowl. Break up the carcass and put in a pan with the giblets, neck and 3 cups cold water. Bring to a boil and simmer half-covered for at least 30 minutes; strain, retaining the liver.

Meanwhile, heat the fat in a frying pan, coat the pieces in seasoned flour and brown them briskly; transfer to a casserole. *Sauter* the vegetables in the same fat and scatter over. Mix the cinnamon into the pan juices, mash the liver and incorporate also; stir in the stock. Break up the chocolate and stir that in too; when melted and smooth, taste and season. Pour enough of the sauce over the portions just to cover, put on the lid and cook in a preheated 350°F oven for 35–40 minutes, or until very tender.

Quail are tasty – and deceptive. Though they look small, two should make a meal for the hungriest, and one is adequate for most people if served properly accompanied.

RIGHT *Pintadeau au Chocolat is a casserole of guinea fowl with carrots and onions, discreetly flavored with cinnamon and chocolate*

*Roasting quails* is easy. Put a dab of butter in each cavity; wrap each bird in a bacon slice and cook as for *palombes rôties* (p. 40) but for less time (quails cooked on a hot spit take about 15 minutes). Use chicken livers to make the paste for the fried bread croûtes: fry them lightly in butter before mashing.

In the hills of France's east and southeast, vast flocks of small birds peck the summers away on ripening juniper berries (others enjoy the wine-grapes!). This gives them an exquisite flavor and so, come autumn, many of them wind up on the table. Though quail are not among these species, their taste combines well with juniper. Here's a quick and easy example:

# Cailles au Genièvre

## QUAILS WITH GIN

Melt about 1 tbsp butter per bird in a large pan, add 2 juniper berries per bird (crushed lightly if dried), then brown each bird all over on a medium heat. Arrange them side by side, turn the heat very low, cover, and cook extremely slowly until done – perhaps 10–20 minutes more. Warm 1 tbsp gin per bird in a small pan, *carefully* set alight and pour over the quail. Remove birds to a warmed serving dish, give the juices a brisk stir and pour over.

Looking for a new way with leftovers? Try this.

# Fricot de Volaille

## POULTRY – OR GAME – FRITTERS

Chop leftover meat very finely. Season well with salt, pepper, nutmeg, fresh chopped herbs, lemon juice and a little oil. Leave in a bowl for an hour or more, turning occasionally to let the flavors mingle; drain.

Prepare a pancake batter and add it gradually to the meat mixture. When the meat is thoroughly coated and binds together, drop spoonfuls into hot fat and deep-fry until crisp and brown. Serve with homemade tomato sauce★.

Finally, a deliciously decorative addition to a cold buffet or summer dinner party. Choose a large young fresh bird.

# Galantine de Volaille aux Pruneaux

## CHICKEN GALANTINE WITH PRUNES
SERVES 10–15

1 cup *prunes*
*Armagnac or other brandy (or brandy and white wine, see recipe)*
1 *plump roaster chicken, about* 3¼ lbs
2 *carrots, chopped roughly*
2 *shallots [or small onions], chopped roughly*
1 *large onion, chopped*
1 *whole onion stuck with a clove*
*salt and pepper*
*bouquet garni*
¼ lb *uncooked ham, finely sliced*
1 lb *unsmoked bacon*
¾ lb *lean boneless pork*
¾ lb *boneless veal*
1½–2 tsp *apple pie spice*
6 *eggs*

Cover the prunes with brandy and soak as necessary. Simmer till plump and pit carefully.

Bone the chicken (or ask your butcher to bone it for you), making sure the skin is kept intact. Break up the carcass; put the bones, vegetables, seasoning and bouquet in a pan, cover generously with water and boil for 1–2 hours to make a strong stock.

Meanwhile, cut the chicken breasts into large strips, and put in a bowl with the ham, one-quarter of the bacon (cut into small strips), the prunes and their liquid. Add a little more brandy – or white wine – to cover, and soak for at least 2 hours.

Make a *farce* by grinding the pork, veal, remaining bacon and chicken meat finely together; add the spice, a little salt, the eggs and the marinade liquid. Mix well.

Lay out a large fine cloth (a piece of doubled cheesecloth or muslin) and stretch the chicken skin carefully on it, inside upwards. Spread with the *farce*, leaving wide borders all around. Lay the marinated meats along the center, arranging the prunes as evenly as possible among the pieces. Fold in the borders and roll up tightly to make a neat parcel, then wrap snugly in the cloth. Tie or sew firmly and weigh.

Put the galantine in a pan into which it fits closely, but without forcing it. Cover with strained stock and bring to a boil; cover and simmer gently for 16 minutes per pound. Drain and leave under a weighted plate until cold and ready to serve in slices.

# Lapins et Gibier à Poil

## RABBITS AND OTHER FURRED GAME

When times were hard the only meat poor peasants were likely to eat was what they could raise themselves – poultry, pork, kid perhaps – or wild game. Many landlords rarely visited isolated estates, and forests were difficult to manage, so poaching was almost a way of life among country people. Today, nearly every *commune* in France has land where the local inhabitants can shoot for the pot in season.

Rare species such as mountain goats (chamois, ibex, izard) are protected, but there are plenty of deer, hares and wild boar still at large in France. These archaic-looking creatures are prevalent even in highly populated regions (Normandy, the Ardennes, Ile-de-France), because they love browsing in crops. We've seen adolescent pigs strolling happily in ripening corn, aware of but evidently unworried by the shouts and excited yelping of a hunting party at the far corner of the same field.

A boar's head mounted alongside the menu at the gate of a country restaurant announces that this delicacy is in season. *Sanglier* is the adult animal, which is usually marinated and stewed as a *civet* or *ragoût*; the younger *marcassin* (up to six months), much more tender, may be roasted or broiled. *Marcassin* hams, cured and smoked and/or dried, are a particularly delicious form of *jambon de pays*. Sometimes, these strange and menacing beasts are farmed at *élevages de sanglier* (boar farms).

# Marcassin à l'Ardennaise

## WILD BOAR WITH CELERIAC
SERVES 6

Venison, pork or lamb roasts may also be treated this way. This recipe is for young tender meat; older lamb, pork and mature venison will need longer cooking.

Cooked marinade* *using at least*
   1 quart *wine (see recipe)*
*leg of chosen meat (see above)*
5 tbsp *oil*
6 tbsp *chilled butter*
1 heaping tbsp *flour*
3 cups *meat stock*
*salt and pepper*
3–3½ lbs *celeriac*
1 *lemon*
½ lb *Canadian bacon, snipped*

Make the marinade, tying the herbs, cloves, juniper and peppercorns loosely together in a cheesecloth. When it has cooled, soak the meat for 1–3 days in a cold place, turning 2–3 times. Drain and dry the meat; strain the marinade.

Cook the marinade vegetables in half the oil and a third of the butter for 2–3 minutes; add the flour and stir until it colors. Blend in the stock and marinade liquid, add the herb bag and seasoning, bring to a boil and simmer steadily until reduced by half, 60–80 minutes.

Meanwhile paint the remaining oil over the meat and roast it in a large pan in a preheated 425°F oven for 20–25 minutes. Peel the celeriac, rubbing the cut edges with a half lemon; cut into coarse dice and sprinkle with lemon juice to prevent browning.

Remove the meat from the pan and pour off any fat. Add just over half remaining butter, the celeriac, bacon, pepper and a *little* salt. Replace meat, return to oven, and reduce heat to 350°F. Finish cooking as usual for chosen meat (cook venison as lamb but baste more often as it has no surface fat might otherwise).

Strain and taste the sauce; finish it by whisking in the remaining butter in tiny pieces (this should be very cold). Arrange the celeriac and bacon on a warmed serving dish and incorporate the pan juices into the sauce. Carve the meat, lay it on the celeriac and spoon a little sauce over; serve the remainder separately.

Leftover celeriac may be puréed, reheated and *lightly* flavored with chopped mint to eat with cold meats.

OPPOSITE *Sanglier (adult wild boar)*
RIGHT *Roast boar served on a bed of celeriac*

A popular way of cooking game animals is to marinate a cut, then roast it using the marinade to make rich gravy: a simple and tasty method, but it leaves the rest of the animal unused. Here are some suggestions for "spare" cuts of venison – or for those who don't wish to cook such a large piece. (*Venaison* is the generic French term for venison; sold and served as *chevreuil*, it is usually roe deer.)

# Côtelettes de Chevreuil à la Forestière

### VENISON CHOPS WITH MUSHROOMS
### SERVES 4–6

Marinate 12 venison chops in a half-quantity of marinade★ made with diced vegetables; remove and pat dry; strain the marinade, reserving the vegetables. Fry the chops in hot lard until nicely browned but pinkish inside; remove and keep hot.

Soften the diced marinade vegetables in the same pan, moisten with a ladleful of marinade liquid and reduce quickly to half. Add ¾ cup tomato sauce★ and leave to simmer.

Meanwhile, lightly *sauter* 1 lb mushrooms in butter or oil. Heap them in a serving dish and arrange the chops around them; pour sauce over and garnish, if liked, with a few chopped gherkins.

A similar recipe from Franche-Comté marinates and cooks chops as above. Then fry 12 small slices of bread in the same pan, adding more fat if necessary. Keep meat and croûtes hot. Brown the marinade vegetables in ½ cup butter, stir in 1 heaping tbsp flour and cook to a brown roux. Add the marinade liquid and its bouquet garni, stir till smooth and cook uncovered for 10 minutes; adjust seasoning and sieve.

Serve chops on the croûtes, and spoon the sauce over or hand separately. Surround with fried mushrooms – or with chestnuts and small onions cooked in stock then drained and browned in butter.

# Escalopes de Chevreuil Grésignoises

### VENISON CHOPS, CÉVENNES-STYLE

4 *thick venison loin chops*
⅓ *quantity marinade★ (optional)*
8 *slices bacon*
6 tbsp *poultry or pork fat*
2½ cups *sliced mushrooms*
1 tbsp *brandy*
1 cup *meat or game stock★*
2 tbsp *port or Madeira*
1 tbsp *chilled butter*
*salt and pepper*

Marinate the chops for about 12 hours, turning several times; drain and wipe dry. Wrap in the bacon slices.

*BELOW Venison Chops with Mushrooms*

Melt the fat in a roasting pan, add the mushrooms, stir, then add the chops and cook in a preheated 400°F oven for 15–20 minutes, basting often; pour off fat. *Flamber* with the brandy. Add the stock and port or Madeira; cook on a high heat for a few minutes spooning the bubbling sauce over the chops until they are done to your liking.

Arrange the chops and mushrooms on a hot serving dish and keep warm. Reduce the sauce for another 2 minutes and whisk in the chilled butter, cut into pieces (this will produce a glossy sauce); taste and season. Pour sauce over chops and serve.

**Note** Dried mushrooms are often used in France during the winter. If you wish to use these mushrooms, soak 1½ oz in warm water for at least 2 hours and drain, reserving ¾ cup of the liquid. Use this to replace half the stock – otherwise follow the recipe.

# Râble de Lièvre à la Navarraise

## SADDLE OF HARE WITH STUFFED MUSHROOMS

SERVES 4–5

$\frac{1}{3}$ *quantity marinade*★
2 tbsp *vinegar*
2 *saddles of hare, together weighing about* 2$\frac{1}{4}$ lbs
$\frac{1}{4}$ lb *unsmoked bacon (optional)*
6 tbsp *butter*
6 tbsp *flour*
*oil for painting*
3–4 *large onions, finely chopped*
$\frac{1}{3}$ cup *finely chopped garlic*
1 tsp *dried thyme*
1 cup *stock*
10 *large open mushrooms*

Prepare the marinade, adding the vinegar. If liked, lard the saddles with bacon, then marinate in a cool place overnight. Remove and dry the meat; set the marinade on a medium heat to reduce by half, then strain, pressing as much as possible through.

Make a roux with 2 tbsp butter and 3 tbsp flour, stir in the strained marinade and bring to a boil; leave simmering, to thicken slightly.

Paint the saddles all over with oil and roast in a preheated 375–400°F oven for 20 minutes or until the meat is tender and the juice from a needle-prick is barely colored.

Soften the onions and garlic in 3 tbsp butter; sprinkle on the remaining flour, and stir in the thyme and half the stock. Simmer to thicken and reduce while the meat cooks, adding more stock as necessary to make a *thick* onion sauce.

ABOVE *Roast Saddle of Hare and a garnish of mushroom caps stuffed with onion sauce*

Meanwhile wipe the mushrooms, remove stalks (which may be used for flavoring stews, soups or omelets), paint lightly with oil and broil or fry. If you have the liver of one of the hares, mash it with a fork and stir it into the gravy.

Serve the hare on a carving dish; spoon onion sauce into the mushroom caps and arrange around the meat. Hand the gravy separately.

**Note** Experts specify "three-quarter" hares for this – yearlings that have just reached full growth but not maturity. You can tell a hare's age by its ears: young ones tear easily. If you suspect your hare of being over-age, cook for longer at lower heat.

When famished, peasants would eat almost anything. In Roussillon I found a Catalan recipe for *civet* of squirrel (no reason why it shouldn't be quite palatable, especially as it was flavored with orange peel). Marmot, shy but still visible in high Alpine valleys, was not much valued for its meat save by a few *montagnards* from around Queyras, but I read in an old Savoy cookbook that its fat had "the reputation, true or false, of alleviating rheumatism."

There were recipes for cooking bear: marinate for 10 days, brown, *flamber* and stew for 6 hours; garnish – somewhat frivolously – with fried onion rings. A more interesting idea is marinated bear paw: stew with bacon, ham and vegetables, then slice, crumb and broil; serve with currant-flavored piquant sauce.

Later the Pyrenean bears were so over-hunted – as trophies, not food – that the survivors retreated over the peaks to the more deserted Spanish slopes. Today, protected as much as the mountain goats in a number of beautiful national parks, they're coming back to France. Indeed, the local wardens have given names to many of them and can almost guarantee you a glimpse of at least one.

The most widespread game animal of all is the rabbit. We've met over forty recipes for cooking it – all super; here are just a few.

# Roulade de Lapin Farci

## STUFFED BONED RABBIT
SERVES 4–6

### For the stuffing
¾ lb *boneless pork (or bulk sausagemeat)*
6 oz *slab bacon*
¼ lb *boneless veal*
*handful soft bread crumbs soaked in milk*
3 *garlic cloves, crushed*
*parsley, thyme*
*salt and pepper*
¼ cup *brandy or* marc
1 *egg*

### The rabbit
1 *large, whole rabbit, boned (remove the head, forelegs and lower back legs; your butcher should do this for you on request)*
*slices of bacon*
2 tbsp *oil*
¼ cup *diced bacon*
1 *carrot, sliced*
1 *onion, chopped*
3 *garlic cloves, finely chopped*
*thyme*
½ cup *white wine*

Grind half the stuffing meats, dice the rest; mix all the stuffing ingredients together, bind with the egg and stuff the rabbit, sewing the meat around the stuffing to make a neat T or Y shape. Wrap completely with bacon.

Put the oil and diced bacon in a pan or Dutch oven into which the rabbit will fit closely; add rabbit, cover tightly and cook very gently for 30 minutes. Add the vegetables, garlic and thyme, re-cover and cook for 1 hour longer or until the rabbit is tender right through; remove it and keep warm.

Pour off any excess fat and stir the wine into the pan. Boil briskly, stirring, for a few minutes to obtain a good sauce; check seasoning. Serve in thick slices with the sauce poured over.

LEFT *Stuffed Boned Rabbit, trussed into a Y shape, ready for cooking*

ABOVE *Rabbit with Red Peppers*

Or start with a basic rabbit stew. Soften chopped onions in fat. Brown well-floured pieces and add onions and seasoning. Then choose from the following variations (or make up your own) before covering with wine, light stock⋆ or water and simmering till tender:

*Lapin à la Flamande*: soaked, pitted prunes, fried bacon, raisins; perhaps with beer as its liquid.
*Lapin Provençal*: diced bacon, crushed garlic, herbs and plenty of chopped tomatoes (reduce other liquid accordingly).
*Civet aux Câpres*: garlic, herbs, tomato paste, olives and capers.
*Lapin à la Moutarde*: 4–6 tbsp Dijon-style mustard (thicken further with a *beurre manié* if liked).
*Lapin aux Anchois*: garlic, chopped anchovy fillets.

# Lapin aux Poivrons

## RABBIT WITH RED PEPPERS
SERVES 4–5

1½ lbs *boned rabbit*
¼ cup *diced bacon*
2 tbsp *olive oil*
2 *large ripe tomatoes*
1 tbsp *flour*
½ cup *dry white wine*
*salt and pepper*
*sprig fresh thyme*
2 *broken bay leaves*
2 tbsp *chopped parsley*
3 *garlic cloves, crushed*
*chicken stock⋆ (see recipe)*
4 *sweet red peppers, quartered*
*large slices of fried bread*

Cut the rabbit meat into smallish pieces; brown these briskly with the bacon in the hot oil, remove with a slotted spoon and put aside.

Skin, seed and roughly chop the tomatoes and add them to the pan, stirring and crushing them until they collapse. Stir in the flour, moisten with the wine and reduce briskly by half. Add the seasoning, herbs and garlic, replace the meat and stir; add enough stock to half cover. Cook gently, covered, for 20 minutes; add the peppers and cook for a further 20 minutes, shaking the pan from time to time to prevent sticking. Remove the lid towards the end to thicken the sauce if necessary.

Serve heaped on slices of fried bread, decorated with peppers.

# Viandes: Agneau, Bœuf et Veau, Porc et Jambon, les Abbattis

### LAMB, BEEF AND VEAL, PORK, VARIETY MEATS

The French peasantry remained poor, even poverty-stricken in some areas, well into the nineteenth century or even later. This was partly due to mismanagement of land by aristocratic owners (and by the State which took it over after the revolution); common land was often forest or scrub, which the rich were unwilling and the poor unable to clear and cultivate. The result: inadequate agricultural production to support a huge rural population.
In addition, most "farmers" held tenure under a feudal system whereby they had to provide their masters with stipulated quantities of produce (rather than a proportion) – which frequently meant that there was barely enough left over for the family to live on, let alone to sell for gain.

Many families were able to keep pigs; foraging for themselves and fed on meager scraps, they were inexpensive to rear and provided welcome meat. Whole meat animals were otherwise rarely available to the farmer – though he might be allowed some of the lesser cuts which his *seigneur* didn't want, and the odd goat or superannuated ewe. Consequently the housewife learned to make full use of all parts of an animal – a talent which, incidentally, is still in evidence. Recipes survive today for all sorts of feet, tails – and ears!

# Daube Victorine

### JELLIED BEEF TERRINE
SERVES 8–10

3 lbs *boneless rump, top round or fresh brisket roast*
2–3 *garlic cloves, quartered*
1–2 *thick slices bacon*
2 tbsp *oil*
2 tbsp *cooking fat*
12 *small onions, peeled*
*handful shallots, peeled and sliced*
1 cup *dry white wine*
1–2 tbsp *brandy*
*salt, pepper, nutmeg*
*bouquet garni*
2 *cloves*
*calf's foot or 2 pig's feet, halved lengthwise and thoroughly scrubbed*
*home-made meat stock (as necessary, see recipe)*
2 lbs *carrots*

With the aid of a small knife, cut slits deep into the meat and push in the garlic quarters; cut some of the fattiest bacon into spikes and do the same with them. Heat the oil and fat in a deep pan with a lid and brown the meat all over; then add the onions, shallots and remaining bacon, diced.

LEFT *Daube Victorine*

ABOVE *In mountain areas, like Savoy, sheep are taken up to high altitude summer pastures*

Heat the wine in a saucepan. Warm the brandy in a ladle and carefully ignite it; pour into the wine and stir until the flames die. Pour this over the meat and add the seasonings, bouquet, cloves and the halves of calf's foot or pig's feet. Set the pan, uncovered, over a low heat and add enough stock or water to bring the liquid halfway up the meat.

Scrape the carrots, cut them into slices, add them carefully to the meat pan and cover tightly. (Seal with thick flour-and-water paste. Ideally the lid should have a depression in the middle to encourage condensation to fall back into the pot.) Cook *very* gently for $4\frac{1}{2}$–5 hours, on the corner of the range if you have one, or in a very low oven – say 285°F. In the latter case, bring the liquid slowly to a boil on top of the range first.

Remove every trace of fat from the top of the stew. Choose a bowl deep enough to take the meat and coat the whole of its inside with a little of the liquid. Chill to set. Carefully remove the carrot pieces and use them to line the bowl neatly. Discard the bouquet and halves of foot, put the meat in the center of the bowl and spoon the remaining contents around it. Pour in the liquid, adding extra stock if necessary to make sure the meat is completely covered.

Leave the bowl in the refrigerator overnight to set into a jelly; keep cold until ready for use. Dip the bowl into warm water for a few seconds, wipe quickly and unmold onto a serving plate. Cut into wedges or slices and serve.

# Epaule Farcie à l'Œuf

## STUFFED SHOULDER
SERVES 6–8

Quantities given are for a shoulder of veal; if you use pork or lamb, increase or decrease the quantities of stuffing ingredients respectively. For these alternatives use different herbs: replace the rosemary and oregano with chopped sage or mint.

4 lbs *boned shoulder of meat (see above)*
*salt and pepper*
3 *hard-cooked eggs*
8 *slices bread soaked in stock*★
1–2 *garlic cloves, finely chopped*
1–2 *onions, chopped and browned in a little fat*
*juice of ½ lemon*
2 heaping tbsp *chopped parsley*
1 tbsp *chopped rosemary or oregano (for veal only, see above)*
*fat and liquid for braising (alternative cooking method)*

Open the meat out and sprinkle the inside with salt and pepper. Roughly chop one of the eggs, squeeze out excess stock from the bread, and mix the two together with the garlic, onions, lemon juice, parsley, herbs and seasoning. Shape the stuffing to a convenient size, put it in the meat cavity and press the remaining two eggs into the center. Pull the edges of the meat together around the stuffing and sew the edges up carefully.

Roast as for any cut of this meat and weight – or braise in wine or stock in a greased, covered pan on top of the range over a gentle heat – basting from time to time. The meat is ready when a deep prick with a fine skewer produces a small colorless dribble of juice.

This dish from Navarre was originally made with mutton (the local hill sheep were kept largely for their milk – which provided a wide range of cheeses). It's a quick and colorful way to serve lamb. If required, make it in advance up to the point where the meat and peppers come together, and reheat thoroughly before completing.

# Sauté d'Agneau à la Navarraise

## NAVARRE-STYLE LAMB
SERVES 6

2 lbs *boned lean lamb (cut into 1½ inch cubes) or 12 trimmed lamb chops (not stewing meat)*
*salt and pepper*
¼ cup *butter*
5 tbsp *oil*
2 *medium-size onions, finely chopped*
1–2 tbsp *wine vinegar*
5 *sweet red peppers, sliced*
1–2 *garlic cloves, crushed*
*cayenne*

Lightly season the meat. Heat the butter with 2 tbsp oil in a wide saucepan and fry the meat until sealed and starting to brown. Add the onions, cover and cook gently for 5 minutes, stirring occasionally to mix. Stir in vinegar, cover, and put to one side.

BELOW *Stuffed shoulder of Lamb*

Heat 3 tbsp oil in a frying pan and *sauter* the peppers for a few minutes. Add the garlic, cover and cook slowly, stirring, for 7–8 minutes. Combine with the meat and onions.

Add a pinch or two cayenne, and taste and adjust seasoning if necessary. Cover pan and simmer for 5–10 minutes, or just until the meat is tender and cooked.

Cooking meat (including game and birds) with fruit not only gave an extra taste to meat which may have been uninteresting on its own, but also provided a pleasing "garnish" when the only other accompaniment was chunks of bread.

BELOW *Navarre-style lamb (top), plus Flemish veal with its three sorts of dried fruit*

# Veau à la Flamande

## VEAL WITH PRUNES, APRICOTS AND RAISINS
### SERVES 5–6

Use a boned roast of veal or pork (leg, loin, etc.) – or pork tenderloin (in which case reduce the cooking time accordingly).

¾ cup *dried apricots*
1 cup *prunes*
*light beer or dry white wine (optional)*
1¾ lbs *meat (see above)*
¼ cup *butter*
*salt, pepper, thyme*
2 cups *veal stock*★
⅓ cup *raisins*

Cover the apricots and prunes with hot water, *light* beer or dry white wine, and soak for *at least* an hour.

Tie the meat up neatly and seal it all over in hot butter in a saucepan. Add the seasonings, thyme and stock. Cover tightly and cook very gently for 25 minutes, turning occasionally.

Drain the apricots and prunes, reserving the marinade; add them to the pan, together with the raisins. If the pan contents are not well moistened, add some of the marinade. Re-cover and cook for a further 30–35 minutes, or until the meat is tender right through. Remove the meat and keep it warm. Cook the pan contents, uncovered, until the liquid has reduced considerably and thickened slightly.

Arrange the fruit around the meat, spoon over some of the gravy and serve the remainder separately.

# Longe de Porc Dijonnaise

## PORK WITH MUSTARD
SERVES 6

2 tsp *black peppercorns*
3–4 tbsp *soft bread crumbs*
1 tbsp *chopped sage ( or* 1½ tsp *dried )*
*salt*
3–4 tbsp *Dijon-style mustard*
3 lbs *pork center or sirloin roast*
3 *small apples*
*butter for frying*
1 tbsp *flour*
1½ cups *dry white wine or hard cider*

**Note** If your roast has skin on, score it with the point of a knife, then remove it together with a good half of the fat beneath. Put it, in a shallow dish, into a preheated 425°F oven for 15–20 minutes to make crackling while you prepare the meat.

Crush the peppercorns and mix them with the crumbs, sage and ½ tsp salt. Smear the mustard all over the meat and carefully press the crumb mixture onto it (coat the fat side first, thickly; use any leftover on the other side).

Place the roast, fat side up, in a roasting pan and cover with foil (this must not touch the meat). Remove the crackling from the oven, lower heat to 375°F and roast the meat for about 2 hours, basting occasionally. For the final 30 minutes, remove foil (and put the crackling back into the bottom of the oven, see **Note** above).

Core the unpeeled apples, slice into rings and fry in a little butter until golden and tender.

When the meat is cooked, remove it to a carving board and keep warm. Spoon off the fat from the pan, add a little flour to the pan juices and stir in the wine or cider to make a gravy.

Carve the meat in slices, pour gravy over and serve garnished with apple rings (and pieces of crackling).

Here is a very different pork recipe. In its original form it used pig's blood as liaison. We can achieve a similar thickening with liquidized liver: it shouldn't make the gravy noticeably granular if you don't let it boil. *Toupine*, by the way, is the dialect word for the handled earthenware casserole it's cooked in.

# Toupine de Pieds de Porc

## PIGS' FEET IN RED WINE

½ cup *pork or goose fat*
4 *pig's feet, split lengthwise and thoroughly scrubbed*
2 *onions, chopped*
1 *garlic clove, crushed*
2 cups *red wine*
500 ml/18 fl oz *brown stock*★
1 tsp *dried thyme and 2–3 bay leaves (or bouquet garni)*
*salt and pepper*
2 tbsp *sugar*
12–15 *tiny onions, peeled*
¼ lb *pork liver*
1 tbsp *red wine vinegar*
¼ lb *salt pork, diced*
*slices of fried bread, cut into triangles*
*chopped parsley for garnish*

Heat the fat in a large frying pan. Add the pig's feet and brown them over a high heat, turning frequently to color them evenly; transfer to a casserole. Fry the onions in the same fat and add them to the casserole. Fry the garlic in the same pan for 1 minute. *Déglacer* the pan with the wine, add the stock and, when boiling, pour this into the casserole. Add the herbs and seasoning, cover and cook in a preheated 350°F oven for 2 hours.

Meanwhile dissolve the sugar in 1 cup water, bring to a boil and add the little onions. Simmer these steadily until the liquid is *much reduced*; then cover and cook as gently as possible, shaking from time to time so that the onions become brown and glazed in a thick dark syrup.

OPPOSITE *Loin of Pork with Mustard*
RIGHT *Toupine de Pieds de Porc, a robust winter stew of pigs' feet slowly simmered in red wine*

Liquidize or grind the liver and push through a sieve to remove any bits; blend in the vinegar.

Cover the salt pork with cold water, bring to a boil and cook for 10 minutes. Drain well, dry the dice, then fry until crisp.

Remove the casserole from the oven; skim off any surface fat and adjust seasoning. Stir in the onions and salt pork dice. Just before serving, add the liver and reheat, stirring to thicken, but take care that it doesn't boil or the gravy will become too granular.

Serve garnished with the fried bread. For a finishing touch dip one corner of each triangle in the gravy and then into chopped parsley.

While we're on the subject of variety meats, I really must give you a few examples of the countrywide French ingenuity with this useful and inexpensive range of meats:

# Ris d'Agneau Rouergats

## LAMB SWEETBREADS
SERVES 2

Soak 1 pound lamb or veal sweetbreads in cold water for 1–2 hours, then boil for 5 minutes in fresh water. Cool in a colander under cold running water and remove any skin, gristle or veins with a sharp knife. Heat 2 tbsp oil with 2 tbsp butter and fry the sweetbreads over a fairly high heat for a few moments, turning several times until lightly browned all over; lower the heat to finish cooking – about 10 minutes more, according to size.

Mix 2 tbsp chopped parsley with 2 chopped garlic cloves (or proportions to taste) and sprinkle over sweetbreads. Serve with lemon wedges.

# Rôti de Foie de Veau

## ROAST CALVES' LIVER
SERVES 4–6

1½–2¾ lbs *calves' liver, in one or two pieces*
*cold milk (optional)*
3 *slices bacon*
1½ cups *small mushrooms* ⎫
2 *large onions* ⎬ *minced or finely chopped*
1–2 *stalks celery* 
3 *slices Canadian bacon* ⎭
*grated rind of* 1 *lemon*
*salt and pepper*
6 tbsp *butter*
¾ cup *heavy cream*
1 *heaping tsp flour*
¾ cup *veal stock*★
*juice of* 1 *lemon*

Pare off the thin membrane coating the liver, and trim away any blood vessels. If you like your liver extra mild, soak it in cold milk for 4–5 hours.

Snip the bacon slices into slivers, make slits with a knife all over the liver and push the bacon pieces into them. Mix the mushrooms, onions, celery and chopped bacon with the grated lemon rind and spread over the bottom of a large baking dish. Lay the liver on this mixture and season with salt and pepper. Melt the butter with the cream and pour over the liver, then put the dish in a preheated 350°F oven. Cook for 15 minutes. Take the dish out, mix the flour with the stock and stir it into the mixture. Replace dish in oven and cook for a further 30 minutes, basting from time to time.

When cooked, arrange the liver on a serving dish and keep warm. *Déglacer* the mixture left in the dish with the lemon juice, then sieve, mill or liquidize it; check seasoning and hand this sauce separately. (For family or more informal occasions, the sauce is perfectly edible left in its "rough" state.)

Cooking liver in this way keeps it extra moist. Pork liver (far cheaper) may be

ABOVE *Lamb sweetbreads, lightly fried and garnished with lemon*

sliced, floured and lightly fried in oil, and eaten Catalan-style: covered with homemade tomato sauce★ mixed with wine-swelled raisins and crispy bacon bits, then scattered with fried croûtons and chopped parsley.

For *Gras Double à la Provençale* (Provence-Style Tripe), soften diced bacon, onions, garlic and several skinned and seeded tomatoes in lard. Stir in herbs (as liked) and the tripe, cut into little strips; season and cover with boiling stock. Half cover and simmer for at least 2 hours. Check the liquid at half-time; add a *little* more if it's disappearing. If there's a lot of thin juice by the end of cooking time, mix a little flour with a ladleful of the liquid, stir this in well, then cook for an extra 5 minutes or so, uncovered. Check seasoning and add some tomato paste if it looks rather pale.

Serve in bowls sprinkled with a *persillade* of chopped garlic and parsley.

# Rognons à la Basquaise

## KIDNEYS WITH SAVORY RICE
SERVES 4–6

3–4 *large onions, sliced into rings*
*milk ( see recipe )*
9 tbsp *oil*
2 *large sweet red peppers, cored, pipped and diced*
2 cups *rice ( white or brown )*
7 cups *stock★ or water*
12 *lamb kidneys*
*salt and pepper*
2 cups *roughly chopped mushrooms*

$\frac{1}{4}$ cup *butter*
*seasoned flour*
1$\frac{1}{2}$ cups *homemade tomato sauce★*

Unless you are using mild, sweet onions, cover the onion rings with cold milk and leave to soak to temper the strong flavor. Heat 2 tbsp oil in a saucepan and sweat the peppers gently, covered, until translucent.

Heat $\frac{1}{4}$ cup oil in a large pan, add the rice and stir until the grains become opaque, then add the stock or water (if using water, season well). Bring to a boil, stirring, then cover and reduce heat. Simmer until all the liquid is absorbed and the rice is cooked – 15–20 minutes for white rice, up to 45 minutes for brown. Keep hot.

Meanwhile, halve the kidneys and remove cores. Season with salt and pepper and cook under a hot broiler for 2–4 minutes each side or to desired degree of doneness.

Cook the mushrooms in the butter. Drain and dry the onion rings if you have soaked them, coat in seasoned flour and fry briskly in 3 tbsp hot oil until crisp and golden.

Mix the tomato sauce with the rice and mushrooms and arrange in a ring around the edge of a large serving dish. Heap the kidneys in the center and sprinkle the peppers over. Decorate the rice with onion rings.

BELOW *Basque-style kidneys cooked with rice, mushrooms, onion rings and red peppers*

# Pot-au-Feu de Langues d'Agneau

## LAMBS TONGUE "STEW"
SERVES 4–6

**For the *bouillon***
¼ cup *butter*
2 *carrots, chopped*
1 *large onion, chopped*
1 *leek, chopped*
1 *bunch of celery chopped*
2 lbs *boned breast or neck of lamb, cut into chunks*
*bouquet garni*
2½ quarts *light stock★*
*salt and pepper*

**The lambs' tongues**
8 *fresh lamb tongues*
3–4 *carrots*
1 *turnip*
8 *whites of leek*
1 foie gras *(Optional. This should be fresh; if you substitute canned* bloc *(not pâté), slice it thickly and add only about 5 minutes before serving.)*

Make the *bouillon* the day before. Melt the butter and quickly fry the vegetables lightly in a very large pan. Add the chunks of meat and brown them too. Add the bouquet garni and stock; bring to a boil, then simmer gently, uncovered, for 2 hours. Strain, taste and season; leave in a cold place overnight.

Meanwhile, soak the tongues in cold water for 1 hour; drain. Put in a pan and cover with fresh water; bring to a boil. Drain again and rinse under cold running water, trimming if necessary.

Remove any trace of fat from the top of the *bouillon*, transfer to a large, clean pan and bring to a boil. Season the tongues and simmer very gently in the *bouillon*. Meanwhile trim the remaining vegetables into neat strips. When the tongues have cooked for 45 minutes, add the vegetable pieces, together with the *foie gras* (see above). Continue cooking for about 15 minutes, or until vegetables are tender but still crisp. Slice the tongues and serve each guest with some sliced tongue, a piece of *foie* and some veg-etable pieces in a soup plate; serve the gravy in a bowl separately.

ABOVE *Lambs Tongue "Stew" may be exotically flavored with foie gras*

*Boudins* are among the seemingly hundreds of varieties of French sausage, and may be white or black. The white ones are sometimes made with chestnuts. The black ones, *boudin noir*, are similar to our blood sausages, and the black puddings of England. That country and France take part in an annual competition in Normandy to judge "the best."

# Boudin à la Normande

## BLOOD SAUSAGE, NORMAN STYLE

Prick the skins of 4 portions of blood sausage. Fry gently, covered, in a little butter, turning occasionally.

Peel, core and chop 2 lbs apples (any type) and cook gently to a thick pulp in $\frac{1}{4}$ cup butter; sweeten if liked. Stir in 3 tbsp Calvados and 6–7 tbsp heavy cream. Spread this mixture in the bottom of a serving dish and arrange sausage pieces on top; garnish with fried bread triangles. Optionally *déglacer* the sausage pan with 3–4 tbsp Calvados to make a sauce, and hand this separately.

ABOVE *Black boudins (sausages) are among the enormous range of charcuterie generally available throughout France*

More simply, skin, split and flour portions of blood sausage, then fry or cook in your usual way. Serve with quarters of apple fried in butter until brown.

# Boulettes de Viande à la Montagnarde

## CHEESE-CAPPED MEATBALLS FROM SAVOY

SERVES 5–6

2 medium-size onions, finely chopped
2–3 garlic cloves, finely chopped
3 tbsp oil
4 slices crustless bread soaked in a little milk or water
1¼ lbs ground beef
1 egg
1 tbsp chopped fresh herbs (or 1 tsp dried)
2 tbsp chopped parsley
salt and pepper
flour for coating
½ lb Beaufort, Gruyère, Swiss or Cheddar cheese

Soften the onions and garlic in a little oil until transparent; take off the heat before they brown. Squeeze out the soaked bread and mix in a bowl with the beef, softened onions, egg, herbs and parsley; stir well and season.

Shape the mixture into a dozen or so small balls and coat them in flour.

Heat the remaining oil (and a little more if necessary) in a frying pan; shake any excess flour off the meatballs and fry for about 10 minutes until brown all over.

In the old days this was finished in the frying pan; I find it easier to use an oven or broiler. Slice the cheese to give one square slice per meatball; lay one on top of each meatball. Cook in a preheated 450°F oven or under a hot broiler until the cheese is melted but not running off. Serve at once. (The meatballs may be browned and cooked in advance. Reheat them thoroughly before adding cheese and finishing.) Serve with tomato sauce★.

A Catalan version of this recipe from Roussillon – Boles de Picolat – cooks the meatballs in a savory sauce: to a half quantity of tomato sauce★ add ⅓ cup diced, cooked ham, ½ tsp ground cinnamon, a pinch of cayenne (or 2 drops hot pepper sauce) and chopped green olives to taste. Cook the meatballs in this after browning them quickly. Omit cheese hats for this variation.

# Bocconcini

## CORSICAN MEAT PARCELS

SERVES 6

6 thin veal scallops or pork tenderloin slices
6 thin slices cooked ham, about the same size
½ lb Gruyère or Swiss cheese, sliced
seasoned flour
oil for frying
¼ cup butter
2 cups roughly chopped mushrooms
1 tbsp chopped fresh sage or ½ tsp dried
3 cups shelled or frozen peas
salt
3 large slices white bread

Pound the meat slices into thin oblongs. Lay on each a slice of ham and a thin layer of sliced cheese, roll them up neatly into parcels and tie securely with thick thread or fine string. Coat the parcels in seasoned flour; heat 2 tbsp oil in a frying pan and fry them briskly until brown. Transfer to a wide saucepan.

Déglacer the frying pan with 2–3 tbsp hot water and pour this over the meat. Melt the butter in the frying pan and lightly sauter the mushrooms. Scatter them over the meat, with the sage. Cover and cook gently for 20–25 minutes.

Meanwhile put the peas into boiling salted water, bring back to a boil, then drain. Add these to the meat pan 5–6 minutes before serving (1 minute for frozen peas).

Cut the bread into 6 rectangles and fry in hot oil till golden. Arrange the croûtes on a warmed serving dish, untie the meat parcels and lay one on each croûte. Surround with the cooked vegetables.

LEFT Corsican Meat Parcels (left) and Cheese-Capped Meatballs from Savoy
RIGHT Le Mounjetado, a spicy bean casserole

*Cassoulet*, that hearty and flavorsome bean stew from Languedoc, engenders almost as many arguments among the experts over its cooking as does *bouillabaisse* from the Mediterranean! This version comes from the old Comté de Foix, in the central Pyrenees.

# Le Mounjetado

## CASSOULET FROM FOIX
SERVES 6–8

2½ cups *dried navy beans*
1 *ham hock*
2 *chorizos or spicy sausages*
1 *onion studded with 3–4 cloves*
1 *bulb garlic, separated into cloves but not peeled*
1 *bouquet garni*
*pepper*
1 *bulb garlic, peeled and chopped*
1 *onion, finely chopped*
2–3 tbsp *fat or oil*
1 lb *tomatoes, skinned, seeded and quartered*
2 *legs* confit d'oie *or* 4 *legs* confit de canard *(p. 109) (optional)*
1 lb *link pork sausages*

Soak beans overnight in unsalted water.

Place the hock in a large pan of cold, unsalted water, bring to a boil and drain. Rinse pan, replace hock; add the spicy sausage, "cloved" onion, unpeeled garlic and bouquet garni; season with pepper. Cover generously with water, bring to a boil and simmer for 2 hours or until the meat begins to fall off the bones. Strain, reserving the *bouillon*.

In a large saucepan, soften the chopped garlic and onion in fat or oil. Add the spicy sausage, cut into pieces, the meat from the hock, the tomatoes and the drained beans; moisten with some of the *bouillon*. Simmer very gently for 3 hours, adding more *bouillon* from time to time to keep it moist. Check seasoning.

Transfer to a casserole (or two); push the *confit* pieces under the surface. Halve the pork sausages, fry until brown and arrange on top. Cook in a preheated 350°F oven for about 1 hour. (It's judged perfectly cooked when the liquid is almost all absorbed and the remainder creams up around the edges of the casserole.)

Cold weather sharpened healthy mountain appetites and the *pots-au-feu* of central France were augmented by vast "dumplings" cooked in the same pot as the meat and vegetables. They had many names, such as the *farcidures* ("hard stuffing" – a misnomer if ever there was one) of Limousin and the *miques* of Périgord. Choose from one of the two *mique* recipes below.

*Pot-au-feu* is an all-embracing term for a big dish of meat simmered with plenty of vegetables to make a two-course meal. The meat may be stewing chicken or other poultry, corned beef or elderly game birds or animals, mutton, goat or salt pork. (Only large pieces are used; small ones may disintegrate in long cooking.)

Quantities given for the following recipes (*pot-au-feu* and one *mique*) will serve 6–8 generously. There's a recipe on p. 133 for salting pork lightly in the old-fashioned way – known as *petit salé*.

# Pot-au-Feu

SERVES 6–8

Prepare 2¼ lbs meat (rinse or soak salted meats as described for *petit salé* or according to butcher's instructions). Calculate its cooking time and relate it to the rising and cooking times for the chosen dumpling (see below), so that they are both ready at the same time and you have a timetable from which to work.

If using *petit salé*, after rinsing/soaking, put it into a large pot and cover with cold water; bring to a boil and poach for 5 minutes. Taste the water: if it is *very* salty, discard it and start again. It should be poached in total for about 2–2½ hours according to the thickness of the cut. Cook other meats as you would if you were boiling them for any other purpose. If using *mique*, remember to add it at the appropriate time.

Forty-five minutes before the end of cooking, add some prepared vegetables, cut into serving pieces; perhaps 1 head of cabbage, 4–6 carrots, 4 large potatoes, 2 turnips, 5–6 leeks.

When the meat is quite tender and the vegetables are cooked, lift the *mique* out carefully; strain the stew. Serve the meat, vegetables and *mique*; the *bouillon* or stock may be served as a soup before the meat and vegetables or as a gravy, or kept as a basis for future soups.

BELOW *Pot-au-Feu of beef, served with a huge bacon-flavored bread dumpling*

# Mique Levée

## LIMOUSIN/QUERCY DUMPLING
SERVES 6–8

Mash 1 cake (0.6 oz) compressed yeast in 5 tbsp warm water and leave in a warm place to froth up.

Meanwhile, sift 2 cups flour and $\frac{1}{2}$ tsp salt into a large bowl. Make a well in the center and break in 2 eggs, one by one, stirring all the time with a wooden spoon, gradually drawing in the flour. Continue stirring and add 2 tsp oil or melted goose fat spoonful by spoonful, then the yeast mixture. As mixture thickens, discard the spoon and use your hand to mix. Add a little more warm water or stock to make a fairly firm but not stiff dough.

Knead very well, then leave the dough in a warm place to double in size and develop surface splits (2–4 hours).

Carefully add the *mique* in one piece to the *pot-au-feu* 1 hour before the end of its cooking time. After 30 minutes turn it carefully.

Traditionally this *mique* is divided with two forks – not cut with a knife, which could squash it and destroy its lightness.

# Mique du Sarladais

## BREAD DUMPLING
SERVES 6–8

Lightly fry $\frac{1}{3}$ cup bacon in 3 tbsp pork or goose fat. Moisten 3 cups diced day-old bread with just enough *pot-au-feu* stock to break it down into a sponge-like consistency. Blend 1 cake (0.6 oz) compressed yeast with 2 tsp warm *pot-au-feu* stock; work this into the soaked bread.

Blend in 3 beaten eggs and the bacon plus its fat; mix well and adjust the seasoning. If necessary add more stock to make a *medium* dough. Shape into one oval dumpling; leave to rise for 45 minutes in a warm place. Add to the *pot-au-feu* 30 minutes before serving.

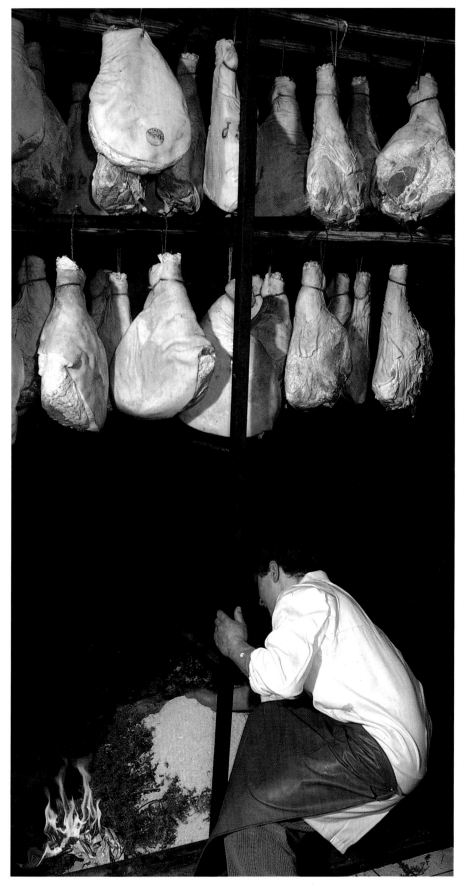

RIGHT *Smoking Jambon de Pays. Juniper is cast onto the flames to add flavor*

# Légumes et Salades

## VEGETABLES AND SALADS

Country folk, even today, are not great salad eaters – perhaps considering greenstuff as animal fodder. For poor peasants, cooked vegetables were more often a meal in themselves (especially if they were dried legumes), or the main ingredients in soup, rather than an accompaniment to the seldom-eaten meat.

The British used to be notorious (fortunately less so nowadays) for overcooking vegetables, especially green ones. I can report that it was a universal ignorance of vitamins – not just their Britishness – which caused this abuse. Nearly every old French recipe I have come across has the same fault, and I have therefore cut the cooking times in many of the recipes in this chapter. (Of course if a vegetable is baked it may take longer to cook, or it may be more suitable to the dish when cooked to a creamy tenderness.)

The Conquistadors brought the potato to Spain in the sixteenth century, but its use was slow to spread. Though European botanists studied it, they considered it more a horticultural curiosity than a food. Famines were often due mainly to a shortage of bread, and early experiments concentrated on trying to make a potato flour suitable for baking. It was the eighteenth-century Frenchman Parmentier who gained royal support and backing for

BELOW *An appetizing display of vegetables*

research in practical potato growing and cooking. (On their birthdays Louis XVI wore potato flowers in his buttonhole, and Marie-Antoinette dressed them in her hair!) Further food shortages accelerated popular interest in potatoes after the Revolution, though the Savoyards – not yet French at that time – had taken them up much earlier. It took a surprisingly short time after that for these homely vegetables to appear in most European kitchen gardens.

Here's an attractive way of serving them, especially if you already need a hot oven. To save washing dishes, you could profitably heap the center with another vegetable (e.g. peas) or even with sausages, meatballs, etc.

# Couronne de Pommes de Terre

## POTATO CROWN
SERVES 4–6

3 lbs *potatoes, peeled and very coarsely grated*
1 *large onion, sliced*
1–2 *garlic cloves, chopped*
*salt and pepper*
1–2 tbsp *flour*
5 tbsp *butter*
½ tsp *paprika*
¾ cup *cream*

Mix the prepared potatoes, onion and garlic in a large bowl, seasoning well. Sprinkle in the flour, 1 tsp at a time, turning the mixture with your hands just until it starts to become sticky.

Grease a large ring mold with some of the butter; transfer the potato mixture into this. Press down *very lightly* and dot with the remaining butter. Cook in a preheated 400°F oven for about 50–60 minutes.

Meanwhile stir the paprika into the cream and heat without boiling. Unmold the cooked potato ring onto a heated serving dish and spoon the cream over it to soak into the mixture.

RIGHT *Couronne de Pommes de Terre*

For *Pommes de Terre Lyonnaises* peel 3 lbs potatoes and cut into coin-thick slices; rinse and dry thoroughly. Toss in ¼ cup of oil to coat; add 3 large chopped onions. Cook steadily over medium heat, turning carefully with a spatula from time to time to prevent sticking. (Add a little more oil during cooking if really necessary, but all the fat should be absorbed by the time the vegetables are done.) When tender and golden brown, season to taste and top with chopped parsley.

*Trouffade Auvergnate*, though lavishly served with mountain ham in its homeland, is almost a meal in itself. Melt ⅓ cup diced fat bacon in a heavy frying pan until the fat runs and it starts to brown; add 1 lb peeled, rinsed and sliced potatoes, seasoning, and 1 cup diced semi-soft or shredded hard cheese. Stir well, then cover and cook gently for 20–25 minutes, pressing the top down occasionally so that it sticks together to form a cake. Check with skewer that potatoes are done; invert onto a warmed serving dish, revealing a crisp brown top.

*Le Fricot* is an unusual Dauphinois accompaniment for game, blood sausage or mutton. Cut 6 large peeled potatoes into ¾ inch dice and cook in 2 tbsp oil and ½ cup butter for 2 minutes. Stir in a heaping tbsp flour, season with salt and pepper and moisten with ¾ cup water or light stock★; cook very gently for 20 minutes. Meanwhile, peel and core 6 pears and slice each one into 8 pieces. Add them to the potatoes after 8–10 minutes, adding a *little* more water or stock if they begin to stick.

From Franche-Comté comes an intriguing Hot Potato Salad. Boil scrubbed potatoes for 15–20 minutes until just tender; peel and slice them. Put at once into a bowl with a few finely chopped shallots and 2 tbsp chopped parsley; dress with vinaigrette★, using 1 part vinegar and 1 part wine to 2 parts olive oil. Serve while still hot.

French country wives can even turn "boring" cabbage into something special:

*OPPOSITE For Chou à l'Ardennaise, both red cabbage (bottom) and white (top) may be used. Trouffade Auvergnate (center) is a hearty potato cake*

# Chou à l'Ardennaise

## BRAISED CABBAGE
SERVES 4–6

**Note** Suitable for any cabbage. Use red wine for red cabbage (plus currant jelly and vinegar), white wine for green and white varieties.

1 *medium-size head cabbage*
*salt and pepper*
¾ lb *tart apples*
2 tbsp *oil or lard*
1¼ cups *wine*
2 tsp *juniper berries*

**For red cabbage only**
1 tbsp *currant jelly*
1–2 tsp *vinegar*
*sugar (to taste)*

ABOVE *On the steep slopes of the Rhône, vines march like military Christmas trees*

Quarter and core the cabbage; cook for 3 minutes (5–10 for red cabbage) in boiling salted water. Drain, pressing out all water; shred. Peel, core and dice the apples. Heat the fat in a large stewpan; stir in the apples and cabbage. Season and stir in wine and berries.

Bring to a boil, cover and simmer for 20–25 minutes (or cook in a preheated 350°F oven for 35–40 minutes). Turn occasionally to prevent sticking, adding more liquid if necessary. When the cabbage seems almost ready, check the liquid: if it seems watery remove lid to evaporate excess. For red cabbage, mash the jelly into the vinegar, stir into the cabbage and cook for an extra few minutes. (Red cabbage takes longer to cook than other types – a total of 45–50 minutes, 65–70 in the oven.) Check seasoning and serve hot.

71

# Chou Lyonnais

## CABBAGE WITH ONIONS
SERVES 4–6

Shred 1 head green or white cabbage (about 2 lbs), discarding the outside leaves and stalk. Plunge it into boiling salted water and cook for 3–5 minutes; drain and press out all moisture.

Sweat 3 sliced onions in 1 tbsp each of butter and beef or bacon drippings (or lard); when transparent, turn up the heat to brown slightly. Stir in 2 tsp brown sugar, 1 tsp sea salt and plenty of ground black pepper. Cook until colored a little more, then incorporate the cabbage; reheat. Optionally, sprinkle lightly with caraway seeds to serve.

# Fouson de Chou

## CABBAGE AND BACON BAKE
SERVES 4–6

2 *medium-size onions, finely chopped*
1 tbsp *oil*
⅔ cup *diced slab bacon*
½ *head white cabbage (about* 1 lb*), finely shredded*
2 *garlic cloves, finely chopped*
*salt and pepper*
2 *eggs*
¾ cup *milk*
1 cup *soft bread crumbs*

Sweat the onions in the oil in a large pan for a few minutes, then add the bacon; cook until more fat runs. Mix in the cabbage and garlic; season with pepper and perhaps a little salt, depending on the saltiness of the bacon. Cook for a few minutes until it starts to color. Transfer to a shallow baking dish. Beat the eggs with the milk and pour over. Sprinkle with crumbs and cook in a 325°F oven for 1 hour.

**Note** To make a complete light meal, increase the amount of bacon; mix the bread crumbs with enough grated cheese to make a generous layer on top, and cook as above.

RIGHT *Gratin de Citrouille aux Tomates combines pumpkin with tomatoes, onions and herbs*

# Gratin de Citrouille et Tomates

## PUMPKIN AND TOMATO BAKE
SERVES 4–5

2½ lb *pumpkin, peeled*
6 tbsp *oil*
2 *large onions, finely sliced*
1 tsp *sugar*
1 lb *tomatoes, skinned and sliced*
2 *garlic cloves, crushed*
2 tsp *chopped fresh basil or tarragon (or ⅛ tsp mixed dried herbs)*
2 tbsp *chopped parsley*
*salt and pepper*
⅔ cup *soft bread crumbs*
2 tbsp *butter*

Remove any seeds from the pumpkin and cut it into 2 cm/¾ in wide strips; cook for 2–3 minutes in boiling salted water, drain and dry *thoroughly* on a cloth. Cut into rough dice.

Heat a third of the oil in a large frying pan and cook the onions gently for 5 minutes, then faster to brown them. Stir in the sugar, then add the pumpkin and fry it gently until it starts to turn transparent; lay it in a shallow baking dish. Heat the remaining oil, and add the tomatoes, garlic, herbs and half the parsley to the pan; season well and cook steadily, turning from time to time. When the tomatoes collapse and the moisture has reduced somewhat, spread the mixture evenly over the pumpkin pieces.

Mix the remaining parsley with the crumbs and sprinkle over the vegetables. Dot with butter and bake in a preheated 400°F oven for 20 minutes or until it is nicely browned.

Almost every *potager* (French kitchen garden) grows Swiss chard. Cut from the outside, it keeps renewing itself from the center and is popular for its versatility: the big shiny leaves may be cooked as spinach – though the taste is different – on their own or in soups and stuffings. The long pale ribs are treated as asparagus when they are young and tender, braised when they are more robust.

To accompany plain meat, broiled sausages or boiled ham, try the following. (As so often, more eggs and cheese, plus perhaps a little fried bacon, turn it into a light snack meal.)

# Côtes de Bettes Voironnaise

## CHARD STALK SCRAMBLE
SERVES 6

2 lbs *chard stalks (or other vegetable, see* **Note** *below)*
*juice of* ½ *lemon*
6 tbsp *butter*
*salt and pepper*
1–2 tbsp *light meat stock★*
½ cup *shredded cheese*
2 *eggs*

Wipe and trim the stalks and cut into convenient lengths. Blanch them in boiling salted water and lemon juice until tender but still crisp (5–8 minutes unless rather tough); drain and dry.

Melt the butter in a wide, heavy pan and toss the stalks in it; season well, and add the cheese and stock. Turn frequently to blend and melt the cheese.

Shortly before serving, lightly beat the eggs and pour over. Turn a couple of times with a spatula over a high heat until eggs begin to set. Serve at once.

**Note** The same treatment may be accorded to celery, Jerusalem artichokes, salsify (oyster-plant), turnips, carrots, Belgian endive and leeks. Remember to adapt the initial cooking time to suit your chosen vegetable.

LEFT *Chard stalks (or a number of other vegetables, see* **Note** *above) are cooked with eggs, stock and cheese.*

# Estouffade de Poireaux

## LEEKS IN RED WINE
### SERVES 3–4

1 lb *white parts of leeks (use remainder
  for soup)*
1 tbsp *oil*
2 tbsp *butter*
1 cup *red wine*
*light stock\** *(see recipe)*
*salt, pepper, nutmeg*
*bouquet garni*
6 *hard-cooked eggs*

Cut the leeks into short lengths. Heat
the oil and butter in a large, heavy
covered stewpan and cook the leeks
very gently. (If they are very thick, cut
them lengthwise also, but cook carefully as the bâtons should remain neat.)
Do not brown.

When they start to soften, bring to a
boil enough wine to cover the leeks and
pour it over (add stock to cover if
necessary). Add seasonings and bouquet garni; simmer gently, uncovered,
for 30 minutes or until the liquid is
much reduced. Remove bouquet.

Serve hot – or cold, garnished with
halved eggs.

Wine is also used in this very pretty
cooked salad from Languedoc.

# Salade de Poivrons

## PEPPER SALAD
### SERVES 4–6

Prepare and cut up 2 red and 2 green
sweet peppers, 2 stalks celery, 3 carrots,
4 gherkins (and optionally 1 chili pepper cut *very* fine). Cook them, together
with 12 tiny onions or scallions (sliced
if you prefer), in ½ cup of olive oil for
5–10 minutes. Season with salt and
pepper, pour on 1 cup of white wine
and cook gently. Don't overcook: the
salad should retain its crispness and
glorious colors – say 10 minutes maximum. Chill well, and serve sprinkled
with lemon juice and chopped parsley.

Colorful additions might include
yellow peppers or green beans; sliced
ripe, green or stuffed olives (added
*after* cooking); a very little fennel (remember its strong flavor); skinned *firm*
tomatoes; cooked peas.

TOP *Leeks in Red Wine may be served hot or
cold*
ABOVE *Pepper Salad combines peppers and a
variety of brightly colored vegetables in a
cooked wine dressing*
OPPOSITE *Lettuce and Orange Salad*

The next pretty salad – *Laitue à l'Orange* – really needs small, juicy, thin-skinned oranges (if not available use thicker-skinned oranges and peel and slice them thinly or, better, divide into pithless segments). If the heads of lettuce are tiny, leave them whole. Proportions to suit yourself.

Slice the oranges very thinly, catching the juice; mix them with the washed and well-dried lettuce in a salad bowl. Mix the juice of 2 lemons with any juice from the oranges, $\frac{1}{4}$ cup olive oil, salt and black pepper. Scatter the salad with ripe olives and pour the dressing over; serve at once.

In winter, when lettuce is scarce, surround a heap of ripe olives with the orange slices and dust these liberally with black pepper: perhaps hardly a salad, but a decorative and tasty addition to a winter table.

Though sweet, tender young garden peas are peerless when simply cooked in minted water and served with a pat of butter, it's worth trying one of the classic French methods of cooking them without water. One such – simple and flavorsome – is:

# Petits Pois à la Paysanne

## PEAS WITH ONIONS AND LETTUCE
SERVES 6

Heat 6 tbsp butter in a heavy pan or flameproof casserole; when it froths, add a bunch of trimmed scallions (minus their green tops) and cook over medium heat for 5 minutes. Wash, trim and shake dry a large head of Bibb lettuce and push it, whole, into the pan; cover and cook very gently for another 5 minutes or until it starts to collapse.

Tip 6 cups shelled green peas (from 4 lbs in pod) over the lettuce; lay a bay leaf and a sprig each of parsley and thyme on top (no seasoning yet). Replace lid tightly and continue to cook gently until peas are tender – up to 45 minutes, but check occasionally after 20 (which should be enough if you have substituted frozen peas). The vegetables provide their own steam for cooking.

Remove herbs and, using two spoons, lift the by now rather ragged lettuce out into a heated serving dish. Stir a little salt and pepper into the pan, spoon the peas and onions over the lettuce, then pour on the buttery juices.

Back to the oven for the next dish which (especially if you reduce or omit the bacon) makes a comforting accompaniment to cold meat on a cold day. By increasing the bacon or adding cooked sausage, it becomes a ribsticking meal.

# Haricots Rouges au Montigny

## KIDNEY BEANS IN WINE
SERVES 6–8

1½ cups *dried red kidney beans or* 1 lb
  *drained canned ones*
1 *small onion, finely chopped*
2 *shallots, finely chopped*
6 tbsp *butter*
½ lb *slab bacon, snipped*
1 tbsp *flour*
1½ cups *red wine*
1 cup *stock*★
8–10 *tiny whole onions or small bunch of*
  *scallions (optional)*
1 *medium-size onion studded with 2*
  *cloves*
1 *garlic clove, crushed*
*salt and pepper*
*chopped parsley for garnish*

If using dried beans, soak overnight. Drain, and boil in fresh unsalted water for 1 hour; drain again. If using canned beans, just drain.

Meanwhile soften the chopped onion and shallots in butter. Add the bacon and when the fat is transparent stir in the flour. Pour in the wine and stock and stir until smooth. Add all remaining ingredients except parsley and transfer to a baking dish.

Bake in a 400°F oven for 25 minutes. Serve sprinkled with parsley.

A rather similar bean recipe from Languedoc cooks some white navy beans instead, then stirs in chopped tomatoes, onion and garlic plus seasoning and an enrichment of goose fat. It's cooked in an even hotter oven in order to brown a cheese topping.

OPPOSITE *Delicious bean recipes: Kidney Beans in Red Wine (below) and lima beans with tiny onions, served with crème frâiche*

Talking of beans, Périgord cooks have some good, simple ways with them – perfect foil for some of the rich local dishes.

*Haricots Panachés*, which they like with roast mutton, are green and white beans, cooked separately, drained, then mixed and sprinkled with a *persillade* of chopped garlic and parsley.

They treat *fèves* (fava beans) even more simply. When young and tiny, these are shelled and eaten raw – often as an hors d'oeuvre – with coarse sea salt to dip them into: crunchy and excellent. Older ones are shelled and have the inner skins removed, before being cooked in boiling salted water, barely enough to cover, together with *small* whole peeled onions, a spoonful of sugar and a sprig or two of fresh thyme. Watch carefully: they must neither dry out nor turn mushy – cook for say 12–15 minutes. If they haven't absorbed all the cooking water when they're ready, pour this off carefully before adding freshly ground black pepper and a big spoonful of *crème fraîche*★ or a pat of butter.

BELOW *Vegetables in French markets are always a fresh delight – like these radishes*

The following provençal salad/hors d'oeuvre dish is traditionally served cold – but it is also good lukewarm or even hot in winter (or if you don't have time to chill it).

# Oignons Marinés

## ONION SALAD OR HORS D'ŒUVRE
SERVES 6

**For the coulis (sauce)**
1 lb *tomatoes*
2 *onions*
3 *garlic cloves*
*bouquet garni*
*salt and pepper*
*sprig fresh basil ( or $\frac{1}{8}$ tsp dried)*
$\frac{1}{4}$ cup *olive oil*

**The onions**
2 lbs *small onions*
$\frac{2}{3}$ cup *golden raisins*
1 cup *white wine vinegar*
6 tbsp *olive oil*
*bouquet garni*
*salt and pepper*
*sugar ( see recipe)*

OPPOSITE *A Provençal onion salad which is often served cold as an hors d'oeuvre*
BELOW *Salade Périgordine, with hot bacon*

Roughly chop and mix all sauce ingredients and cook for 30–45 minutes or until soft; sieve.

Peel the onions and put in a stewpan with the *coulis* and all other ingredients except sugar; add just enough water to cover. Stir and bring to a boil. Reduce to simmer; taste. Add sugar, a teaspoonful at a time, to counteract the acidity of the tomatoes and vinegar (the dish should taste slightly sharp, not unpleasantly sour). Simmer, uncovered, for about 1 hour. If onions are not tender, replace lid and cook until they are. (Add a few drops of water if necessary to keep the sauce moist. It should finish fairly thick; if watery, boil briskly, uncovered, to evaporate excess moisture.)

A last word on tomatoes, which make such a pretty garnish on any plate that one hardly needs an extra vegetable. *Tomates Provençales* serve both functions. Cut washed tomatoes in half crosswise and gently squeeze out the seeds. Arrange them on a shallow baking dish, sprinkle with salt, pepper, chopped fresh thyme (or basil) and a little olive oil; cook in a preheated 450°F oven for 15–20 minutes.

Meanwhile make a *persillade* from some finely chopped parsley and garlic (at least one clove for every three tomatoes); mix together. Remove dish from oven, sprinkle with the *persillade* and a few bread crumbs; dribble lightly with olive oil and brown under a hot broiler (photograph, p. 108).

One half tomato makes an attractive decoration, 2–3 serve as a "side" vegetable, 3–4 on their own would be a refreshing appetizer. Delicious hot or cold.

*Cèpes Bordelaises* are a similar idea. Finely chop the stalks of 10–12 large open mushrooms with a small shallot; add a crushed garlic clove, 1 tbsp chopped parsley, 2 tbsp soft bread crumbs, and a pinch or so of salt and pepper. Cook mushroom heads (gills up) slowly in oil, seasoning lightly. After 5 minutes scatter the mixture over, cover and cook for another 5 minutes. Squeeze a few drops of lemon juice over and serve – as a garnish, a vegetable or an entrée (on fried bread croûtes).

The last photograph in this chapter shows *Salade Périgordine*. To each medium to large head of lettuce (keep the leaves whole if small, tear into convenient-sized pieces if large) add 4–6 tomatoes cut in wedges, 4 roughly-chopped hard-cooked eggs and 8–12 broken walnuts. Fry 3 thick slices of bacon, cut in strips, until crisp. Make a vinaigrette*, using walnut oil if possible. Toss the salad in the dressing, add the *hot* bacon pieces and serve immediately.

# Entremets et Desserts

## DESSERTS

There are plenty of luscious French desserts around today, but in the past they were less in evidence – in country houses at least. A meal might finish with fruit from the orchard, or with homemade cheese or a cheese spread (see p. 98). If a sweet item was specially cooked, it was quite likely to be some kind of cake or *pâtisserie* – equally suitable for a mid-afternoon snack – though the addition of cream or custard could transform it into a genuine "dessert." (Do also consult pp. 90–99 for dessert ideas.)

However, important meals – laid on for a wedding or other family occasion or feast day – did include "real desserts," sometimes quite elaborate ones. Here is a selection of some of the various types of dessert to be found in France (excluding ice creams and sherbets which vary more in flavor than in kind from ours).

*Charlottes* are easy to make, and come in many guises. The shell may be slices of sponge cake, ratafia cookies or small macaroons instead of ladyfingers. The filling may be chocolate butter-cream whisked into custard, chestnut purée (vanilla-sweetened, or chocolate- or coffee-flavored), or fruit purées thickened with a little gelatin or arrowroot. If the filling is not very firm, alternate it with layers of the chosen "cake."

A chocolate *charlotte* made with macaroons is called "St Emilion." (Apple charlotte, come to think of it, is made on the same principle, with buttered bread as "cake" and apple as filling. The French have a version too, slightly more adult than ours.)

# Charlotte aux Noix

## WALNUT "CREAM" MOLD

### For the custard filling
2 cups *milk*
5 tbsp *sugar*
*vanilla bean (or few drops extract)*
6 *egg yolks*

3 cups *chopped walnuts*
10 tbsp *butter, softened*
¼ cup *sugar (or to taste)*

### For the syrup
½ cup *sugar*
5 tbsp *rum, brandy or other spirit*

### For the frosting
3 *squares (1 oz each) unsweetened chocolate*
2 tbsp *black coffee or rum (optional)*
9 tbsp *unsalted butter*
1½ cups *confectioners' icing sugar*

18–24 *ladyfingers*
*walnut halves for decoration*

Make the custard for the filling first. Put the milk with a third of the sugar and the vanilla bean (or extract) in a pan; bring slowly to a boil. Meanwhile whisk the egg yolks and the rest of the sugar in a bowl for 2–3 minutes. As soon as the milk boils, pour it onto the egg mixture, still whisking. Return to pan and cook gently, stirring with a wooden spoon or wire whisk to thicken further, but *do not boil*. Strain into a clean bowl and whisk for a few moments longer to avoid lumps. Leave to cool.

Make the syrup: put the sugar in a pan and add rum, brandy or other spirit and ½ cup water. Stir over a gentle heat; when dissolved bring to a boil and cook for 2 minutes. Allow to cool.

Meanwhile grind 1 cup of the walnuts (in blender if liked). Beat the ground nuts with the butter, and sugar to taste; stir in the chopped nuts. Remove the vanilla bean and stir the cooled custard into the nut mixture.

BELOW *Retired folk shelling walnuts from their own trees in Beynac, Dordogne*

ABOVE *Walnut Charlotte, an elegant – and rich – party dessert*

Pour the syrup into a shallow bowl. Dip each side of the ladyfingers (one at a time) *briefly* into the syrup, shake off any excess syrup and use to line sides of a 1-quart charlotte mold or suitable container, then line the bottom; avoid holes by pressing the fingers against the mold, cutting them to fit where necessary. Pour in the walnut cream; it should come to within about $\frac{3}{4}$ in of the tops of the side ladyfingers. Cover the top with more dampened cookies. Place a flat plate or flan ring base over the top and weight lightly; chill for at least 3 hours. Unmold carefully onto serving plate.

To frost, melt the chocolate with the flavoring or 2 tbsp water. Cream the butter until pale and fluffy, then work in the sifted confectioners' sugar. Cool the chocolate (don't let it set) and mix into the frosting until evenly colored. Spread over the charlotte and decorate with walnut halves.

In Rouergue a loop in the Aveyron River washes the base of a spur of rock; the old village of Najac spills along the top, culminating in the ruins of a splendid eleventh-century castle. (Records started about that time, but the town is certainly older.) The huge church was built by the inhabitants in the thirteenth century – as a punishment for being on the wrong (losing!) side in the fearsome Albigensian religious wars.

A family which has been *aubergistes* in this picturesque place for who knows how many generations gave us their family recipe for a traditional and delicious prune pie known as *Pastis aux Pruneaux*:

Prunes are legion in old recipes, probably because of their year-long "keepability." An incredibly simple way of using them has the self-explanatory name of *Noir et Blanc* (black and white). Soak prunes in orange juice as necessary, then pit them. Add shredded orange rind to the marinade and simmer the prunes in it until tender. Flavor with Armagnac (or rum) and chill. Serve very cold with cream cheese beaten with cream and a little sugar, and decorated with more orange rind.

LEFT *The medieval castle overlooking the village of Najac*
BELOW *Alchoholic Prune Pie*

# Pastis aux Pruneaux

## ALCOHOLIC PRUNE PASTRY
SERVES 8–10

### For the *pâte sucrée*
4 cups *flour*
1 cup ($\frac{1}{2}$ lb) *butter*
3 tbsp *sugar*
2 *eggs*
*fat for greasing*
*beaten egg for glazing*

### For the filling
1$\frac{1}{2}$ lbs (about 3 cups) *prunes*
$\frac{1}{2}$ cup *sugar (or less, according to taste)*
3–4 or more tbsp *plum brandy, Armagnac or other spirit*

Soak the prunes as necessary and simmer to plumpness; pit and drain *very* thoroughly. Make a *pâte sucrée*, preferably slightly tough rather than feather-light; chill for 30 minutes.

Generously grease an 8 inch fluted brioche mold. Alternatively use a straight-sided deep cake pan, either spring form or lined with foil to make unmolding easier.

Roll out three-quarters of the pastry dough to $\frac{1}{4}$ inch thick and line the pan with a $\frac{3}{4}$ inch overlap all around. Mix the prunes with the sugar and alcohol (as much as you like but don't make the filling too wet), then pack firmly into the pastry case. Roll out the remaining

dough into a round to make a lid; dampen the edges well, fold in the overlap and press the join hard to seal *really* tightly.

Brush with beaten egg and bake in a preheated 350°F oven for 40–45 minutes. When the top starts to brown and is very firm and the edges begin to come away from the sides, invert the pie very carefully onto a baking sheet. Glaze with more egg and cook upside down for another 20 minutes or so, covering the top if it becomes too brown. Leave until cold before handling further. It's rich and filling, but serve with cream if liked.

Prunes remind me of my childhood, and it is very noticeable how many sophisticated Frenchmen are addicted to old-fashioned nursery puddings. *Flan, Crème Caramel* and *Crème Renversée* are all baked custards and are universal favorites on French menus. *Iles Flottantes* and *Oeufs en Neige* (floating islands and "snowball eggs") are nearly as popular. Even the exotically-named *Négresse en Chemise* is a version (albeit a glamorous one) of chocolate sponge and custard! Here's a recipe for a *very* distant cousin of a familiar and popular childhood pudding:

# Gâteau de Riz au Caramel

## CARAMEL RICE PUDDING
SERVES 6–8

1¼ cups *rice*
*vanilla bean or a few drops extract*
1½ quarts *milk*
1¼ cups *sugar*
9 *egg yolks*

Place the rice in a saucepan and cover with cold water. Bring to a boil and drain.

Add the vanilla to the milk and bring to a boil. Tip in the rice and simmer gently for about 35 minutes (remove the bean after 20 minutes). By this time nearly all of the milk should be absorbed.

In a small pan moisten ½ cup of the sugar with 1 tbsp water. Heat gently, stirring, until quite melted; cook over a

medium heat until it's a rich brown (380°F). Remove from the heat and very carefully add 2 tbsp water (guarding your hands against splashing). Use the caramel to coat the inside of a 10–12 inch ring mold.

Whisk the remaining sugar and yolks together until thick, then stir into the rice. Spoon into the mold and cook in a preheated 350°F oven for 20–25 minutes. Allow to cool slightly then carefully unmold onto a serving dish, chill until ready to serve. Decorate with cream or custard.

Talk of France's favorite desserts must include fruit tarts of all descriptions. There's the *Classic Apple Tart*; which has a base of vanilla-flavored apple purée (cooked in butter) beneath the slices. To get the brown edges which emphasize the apple pattern so attractively, the fruit is sprinkled with sugar and put into a *really hot* oven for a few minutes, then the heat is turned down and it is baked in the usual way.

ABOVE *Caramel Rice Pudding (left), and Noir et Blanc, a wonderfully simple concoction of prunes, cream cheese and brandy*

Another, *Norman Tart*, has an almond-cream filling as well as fruit. Line a 10 inch tart pan with *pâte brisée*★. Cream ½ cup each of butter and sugar until light. Gradually beat in 2 eggs and, optionally, 1 tbsp Calvados or Kirsch. Stir in 1 cup ground almonds and 1 tbsp flour. Spread three-quarters of this into the pastry case and add fruit (pear halves sliced crosswise and laid in a wheel pattern are particularly pretty, but you could use apples). Fill in the gaps with the remaining almond cream. Cook for 10 minutes in a preheated 400°F oven, then for 10 minutes at 350°F. Sprinkle with sugar and lemon juice and continue to bake for another 20 minutes, or until the sugar melts and starts to caramelize. Serves 6. (Photograph overleaf.)

ABOVE *Norman Tart (recipe on previous page) and Orange Cream Tart*

For *Tarte aux Raisins* (grape tart) from Champagne, treat the pastry case as described and bake in advance. Remove it before it's quite cooked and brown. Shortly before serving, pack it tightly with grapes (2 deep if they're small), sprinkle with sugar and bake for 5–12 minutes in the hottest possible oven to melt the sugar and heat through. (Protect the pastry with foil if you fear it might scorch.)

# Tarte à l'Orange

## ORANGE CREAM TART
SERVES 4–6

pâte brisée★ *(make half given quantity)*
1 *thin-skinned orange*
1 cup *sugar*
1¼ cups *orange juice*
2 tbsp *Grand Marnier or other orange liqueur (optional)*
¼ cup *butter*
3 tbsp *flour*
1 *egg*
¼ cup *heavy cream*

Make the pastry dough, roll out and line a 6–7 inch tart pan. Chill.

Blanch the orange in boiling water for 10 minutes; drain and cool; cut into thin slices. Heat ¾ cup sugar in the orange juice and stir until dissolved; simmer the orange slices in this syrup for 25–30 minutes, until skin becomes translucent. Remove them carefully and continue to reduce the syrup until a small spoonful left to cool on a saucer forms a skin. Leave the syrup to cool for a few minutes, then very carefully (it will splutter) stir in the liqueur.

Cream the butter with the remaining sugar. Beat in the flour, then the egg. When smooth, stir in the cream.

Spread the mixture into the pastry case and bake in a 350°F oven for 40–45 minutes until firm; cool.

Arrange the orange slices on the filling and cover with the thickened syrup. (Alternatively, pour on the syrup and lay the orange slices on top – either way is good.) Serve cold.

Make *Tarte au Citron* the same way, using 2 lemons; increase the amount of sugar as necessary (depending on the sweetness of your tooth).

A tip to stop tarts becoming soggy: if baking blind★, that is unfilled, remove the foil and beans after 10 minutes and brush the bottom with lightly beaten egg white (and sprinkle with sugar if liked); finish baking as usual. For cold tarts, simply rub inside the bottom of a *cooled* pastry case with butter after baking blind. This technique works well for strawberry or raspberry tarts; such fruit is also often laid on a bed of *crème pâtissière★*. If baking the contents with the pastry, brush with egg white 15–20 minutes before filling and baking.

A rather unusual pear pie comes from central France. In Berry it's called *Le Poirat*, in Bourbonnais *Picanchagne* (or *Piquenchagne* – from *piqué en chêne*, though I've not yet discovered the explanation).

# Poirat du Berry

## CREAMY PEAR PIE
SERVES 6–8

1½ lbs *firm pears*
*vanilla bean (or extract)*
¾ cup *sugar*
¾ cup *pear brandy, Cognac or rum*
pâte sucrée★ *(to which a pinch of
  cinnamon has been added)*
*beaten egg white*
*beaten egg for glazing*
*sugar for sprinkling*
¾ cup *heavy cream*

Peel, core and quarter the pears, place in a bowl with the vanilla bean and cover with the sugar and spirit; soak for at least 1 hour.

Make *pâte sucrée* and chill for 30 minutes. Roll out two-thirds of the dough and line a 9–10 inch pie pan. Brush interior with egg white and chill again for 5 minutes. Arrange in it the *well-drained* pears in a wheel pattern, filling any spaces with the remaining pears, sliced. Roll out the rest of the dough to fit the top, cutting a 2½–3 inch hole in the center. Brush around the edges with water and seal the lid on; glaze with beaten egg and sprinkle with sugar. Bake in a preheated 350°F oven. Inspect after 45 minutes: if pears are tender and pastry brown, remove pie, otherwise cook for 5–10 minutes longer. Keep warm until ready to eat.

Lightly whip the cream; remove the vanilla bean from the pear marinade and lightly beat the latter into the cream. (If you haven't used a bean, flavor the cream with a few drops of vanilla extract.) Just before serving, pour as much cream mixture as possible carefully into the center hole, making sure that none spills out over the pastry lid. Serve any excess cream mixture separately.

RIGHT *Le Poirat du Berry, a pie filled with rum flavored pears and cream (which is added after baking)*

LEFT *Clockwise from top: Red Fruit Salad, Poires Belle Angevine and Cœurs à là Crème* ABOVE *Almond stuffed figs*

In such a large country as France the climatic variations mean that fresh fruits are in season for much of the year; no wonder that they're so popular for desserts. Little or no effort transforms simple fresh fruit into a "made" dessert.

A supremely simple example is *Salade de Fruits Rouges* (Red Fruit Salad). For 6 servings, dissolve ½ cup sugar (or to taste) in 1 cup each light red wine and water (heat if necessary). Prepare about 1 pint each raspberries and redcurrants; peel, pit and quarter or slice 3–5 peaches. Arrange the fruit in a serving bowl and pour the cooled syrup over, adding more water if necessary, to cover. Leave to steep for a few hours or overnight. Serve chilled with heavy cream. (Loganberries, boysenberries, pitted cherries and/or strawberries can also be used, but the latter should only be left to steep for 1–2 hours.)

In ancient times there was a sweet soup, strangely named *la rôtie* ("the roast"), in which bread and honey were simmered in red wine. This curiosity was later adapted in the Loire valley to make *Chicolle*, which is a sort of follow-on from the marinated fruits above. Peel and pit one ripe peach per person and cut into thin slices. Lay them in a bowl and sprinkle with sugar to taste. Cover with slightly diluted red wine and weight with a plate or saucer to keep the fruit under the liquid. Refrigerate overnight.

Serve very cold with a slice of lightly toasted white bread or 2 ladyfingers per person; these may be dipped in the juice – or crumbled into it to revert to the old "soup" idea.

For *Poires Belle Angevine*, core peeled pears carefully from the base but leave stalks on. Poach them in a syrup made from red wine and sugar to taste, infused with a cinnamon stick and a bruised strip of lemon peel. When tender, cut a slice off the base of each, set them upright in a shallow serving bowl and reduce the syrup until thick but not caramelized. Cool, and correct the sweetness with lemon juice or more sugar; spoon over the pears and chill. Sprinkle with pear brandy, if liked, before serving.

The stuffing for *Figues Fourrées* is best made with *fromage blanc*; if you can't get this, beat cottage or cream cheese until smooth, then whisk it to softness with a little lightly-whipped cream. To stuff 8–10 figs, mix 1 cup ground almonds with 1 tbsp sugar, and bind together with 2–3 heaping tbsp of the cheese (the paste should be quite soft but hold its shape – adjust the texture by adding more cheese or almonds). Taste, and add more sugar if liked (remember the sweetness of the figs – I sometimes add a few drops of lemon juice).

Snip off the fig stalks and split them down from the top as though to quarter them, but don't cut right through. Gently spread the quarters apart and spoon or pipe the filling into the center; top each with a whole almond.

ABOVE *Goats' milk cheeses dry out in the open air, well protected from insects and birds*

A word about cheese. There are traditionally 365 French cheeses – one for each day of the year. It's impossible to count: the official tally is "over 300," but there are certainly many more than that. Made with milk from cows, goats or ewes, French cheeses may be hard, tangy, creamy, mild or pungent; we've yet to find one we didn't like.

Not unnaturally the cheeseboard is an important part of every French menu (even on the cheapest ones it's frequently offered as an alternative to the dessert). Personally, I find the French habit of eating cheese *before* a sweet a good one; it gives an ideal opportunity to finish off your wine which – especially if it's a red one – won't taste good with your dessert. Because the French respect their cheeses (all cheeses are famous in their own district), crackers or highly-flavored rusks are rarely served with cheese, which is normally eaten with a knife and fork, with only bread (not butter) as accompaniment.

Very fresh cheese (*fromage frais* or *fromage blanc*) is sometimes featured. It may be sprinkled with a *persillade* (chopped parsley and garlic – like this it can be served as an appetizer too) or with sugar and cream.

Such cheese is also delicious with fruit – as are the lovely creamy little concoctions called *Crémets d'Angers* (if these are made in heart-shaped molds they're known as *Cœurs à la Crème*). These should be started 1 day ahead. For 6 people, beat $\frac{3}{4}$ cup cream cheese with a fork until smooth and rather soft. Add 1 cup whipped cream a little at a time, mixing well with a fork or wire whisk. Beat 3 egg whites until they hold soft peaks, and gently fold into the mixture. Line 6 porcelain *cœur* molds (available from specialist kitchen stores) or small metal cheese molds, or a heart-shaped cake pan (pierce drainage holes in the base) with cheesecloth and spoon the mixture in. Leave until shortly before serving, then unmold and sprinkle with vanilla sugar. (Picture on p. 86.)

Finally, two slightly unexpected desserts. *Clafoutis*, a sweet batter dessert, is traditionally made with sweet cherries, but sweet-sour would be just as good (you may need a sweeter batter for them). Prunes (pre-simmered and drained), plums, apricots, greengages and so on are also sometimes used. All fruit should be pitted before cooking but is otherwise best left whole to prevent too much juice escaping.

# Clafoutis aux Cerises

### BAKED CHERRY PUDDING
SERVES 4–6

*butter for greasing*
1½ lbs *Bing cherries, pitted*
4 *eggs*
*salt*
½ cup *sugar*
½ cup *flour*
5 tbsp *butter*
1 cup *milk*
*sugar for sprinkling*

Generously butter a wide, shallow baking dish and arrange the cherries evenly over the bottom. Beat the eggs lightly in a large bowl; beat in a pinch of salt and the sugar. Sift in the flour gradually, still beating. Melt two-thirds of the butter and beat it in. Stir in the milk.

Pour this batter over the cherries and dot with the remaining butter. Bake in a preheated 400°F oven for 35–40 minutes, until the batter is set. If you don't want to serve immediately, it may help to prevent the batter sinking if you turn the oven down to 325°F and bake for a few minutes longer. Sprinkle with sugar and serve hot or lukewarm, with cream.

*Papin* is a custard tart, differently flavored from the American favorite. It comes from the Boulogne area and was classically made with a yeast pastry shell, but this seems unnecessary and gives a rather heavy pudding.

BELOW *Clafoutis, a cherry pudding made with a rich egg batter*

# Papin

### HERBY CUSTARD TART
SERVES 4–6

Make some plain or sweet pie pastry (*pâte brisée*★ or *pâte sucrée*★) using only 1¼ cups flour and adjusting other proportions accordingly (alternatively use store-bought pastry). After resting the pastry, roll out and line an 8–10 inch pie pan.

Tie 2–3 sprigs of fresh thyme (or a heaping tsp dried) loosely in cheesecloth, put in a pan with 1½ cups milk and bring to a boil; leave to infuse for at least 10 minutes.

Stir 2 egg yolks into ¼ cup sugar, sift on 6 tbsp flour and mix well. Add the milk, little by little, to make a smooth cream. Transfer to a pan (include the herb bag) and cook gently, stirring continuously, until thick enough to coat the back of a spoon. Leave to cool; remove the herb bag.

Pour the custard into the pastry case and bake in a preheated 400°F oven for 25–30 minutes or until the custard is set and golden brown. Serve cool.

# Pour le Goûter

## SNACK RECIPES

Defined by my dictionary as "a light repast (in the afternoon)," *le goûter* is what French children eat when they get home from school. It's sometimes just a *tartine* (literally "spread"): bread with jam or homemade cheese or – in Périgord and Alsace – perhaps roast-goose fat.

Today children in isolated districts may have to walk (or cycle) some distance to pick up the school buses. Once they'd have walked all the way to school, but despite this trek, farm children had to pull their weight when they got home, especially in times of maximum work – haymaking, harvest and so on. If *maman* was out in the fields, she might leave them a slice of home-cured ham, or some half-prepared snack which the eldest could complete for the rest before they all turned out to help.

Afternoon tea in the English tra-dition is only normally eaten by French families of some pretension (who call it "*le five-o'clock*"). Recipes in this chap-ter comprise some *goûter* snacks, some feast-day traditions, and some sweet things which would be equally good with tea or as a dessert.

We were once lucky enough to be given an old-style Périgordian meal in a private house. It was *Toussaint* (All Saints' Day), when flower-laden French families visit the cemeteries *en masse* to honor their dead. After many delicious courses we just managed to find room for:

# Millia

## PUMPKIN CAKE
SERVES 4–5

**Note** Cornmeal has a slightly gritty texture, and augments the pumpkin color. Rice flour as a substitute would provide texture but not color; use a double quantity of all-purpose flour if you prefer.

$\frac{3}{4}$ lb *pumpkin*
*salt*
$\frac{1}{2}$ cup *sugar*
$\frac{1}{4}$ cup *butter, softened*
*few drops vanilla*
2 tbsp *rum (or Grand Marnier, in which case omit vanilla)*
$\frac{1}{2}$ cup *milk*
2 *eggs, separated*
1 cup *wheat flour*
$\frac{3}{4}$ cup *cornmeal (see **Note** above)*

Preheat the oven to 475°F. Seed the pumpkin, peel and cut into chunks. Cook in boiling, lightly salted water until tender (7–10 minutes). Cool and drain, pressing out *all* moisture; mill, sieve or liquidize. Mix in the sugar, butter, flavoring(s), milk and egg yolks. Beat the whites stiffly and fold in. Mix the flour and cornmeal together and sift onto the mixture, a very little at a time, turning gently with a spatula until it binds together (this may be before all the flour is used, if the pumpkin was well dried).

Pour into a lined deep 8 inch cake pan and put it into the oven. Lower the heat to 400°F and bake for 45 minutes or until a skewer comes out clean. Allow to cool slightly then unmold. Serve lukewarm.

Pumpkins were easily grown (or cheap to buy) and versatile in their uses. They could be the basis of vegetable dishes (see p. 73), of jam (p. 110) or, used to make sweet or savory snacks:

# Beignets au Potiron

## PUMPKIN FRITTERS
SERVES 5–6

1 lb *pumpkin*
*salt*
$\frac{1}{2}$ cup *hot milk*
$\frac{2}{3}$ cup *cornmeal*
6 tbsp *sugar*
$\frac{1}{8}$ tsp *baking soda or baking powder*
1 *egg*
*oil for frying*
*sugar for serving*

Peel the pumpkin, remove seeds, chop roughly and cook in boiling salted water until tender (about 10 minutes). Drain very thoroughly, purée and leave in a warm place to dry out.

Pour the almost boiling milk onto the cornmeal; mix well. Combine with the pumpkin and add sugar and salt to taste. Sprinkle in the soda or baking powder, mix well, and beat in the egg. Leave for about 2 hours.

Deep-fry spoonfuls of the batter until crisp and golden – they will not puff up very much. Drain on paper towels and serve hot, sprinkled with sugar.

(Alternatively, and for a more nourishing snack, omit the sugar and substitute grated cheese, both in the mixture and for sprinkling afterwards.)

These fritters may also be served as a vegetable instead of potatoes: simply omit the sugar and season well with salt and pepper.

OPPOSITE *The bright color of Millia (Pumpkin Cake) is produced by a combination of pumpkin purée and cornmeal*
LEFT *There are many varieties of pumpkins. These bright ones are potirons photographed in the Lot region of southwest France*

RIGHT *These pastry fritters, known as Bugnes, are popular during Lent in Franche-Comté*

Fritters and fried pastries (quick and easy to make) are still popular all over France. The city of Albi is famous for *jeannots* (hard triangular pastry biscuits flavored with *anis*). All across the southern third of the country you find *oreillettes* (meaning "little ears") – small diamond shapes of rum-flavored *feuilletée*★, deep fried till they curl up like piglets' ears. These are traditional during Lent in Provence; in the south-west they appear for the Feast of the Kings (or Twelfth Night), flavored with Armagnac. On Palm Sunday, Périgord children carry horn-shaped fritters, *les cordonelles*, with their palms and box sprays. In Franche-Comté, Shrove Tuesday brings its crop of:

# Bugnes

## PASTRY FRITTERS
SERVES 4–6

Sift 2 cups flour into a bowl with $\frac{1}{2}$ tsp each of salt and baking powder and 6 tbsp sugar; make a well in the center. Stir into this $\frac{1}{4}$ cup softened butter or 3–4 tbsp oil, 2 eggs, 2 tbsp Cognac or rum and a grated orange rind. Gradually draw in the flour from the sides to make a soft dough. If it seems too sloppy to handle, sift on a little more flour: it should be very soft but manageable. Knead lightly on a well-floured board, and chill until firm.

Roll out very thinly ($\frac{1}{8}$ inch thick) and cut into 5 inch diamonds. Make a short lengthwise slit in the center of each and pull the two end corners through the slit, in opposite directions. Deep-fry in very hot oil. They will rise almost at once, but leave for 1–1$\frac{1}{2}$ minutes before turning over to brown the other side. Drain on paper towels and sprinkle with sugar while still hot. Eat hot or warm.

Every region has its variously flavored and shaped *merveilles* (literally "marvels"), all fairly similar to *bugnes*. There are also acacia-flower fritters and, if these flowers are growing in your garden, you could make:

# Beignets de Fleurs d'Acacia

## ACACIA FLOWER FRITTERS
MAKES 20

Mix 1$\frac{1}{4}$ cups flour, 1 egg yolk, a pinch of salt, 2 tbsp olive oil and enough light beer or soda water to make a very light batter of medium cream consistency. Optionally flavor with 2 tsp orange-flower water and/or brandy. Leave for about 2 hours.

Pick at least 20 well-scented flowers (preferably in the early morning), when they have just come into flower. Wipe (or wash if dusty) very gently, leaving an inch of stalk as a "handle." Stir the batter and fold in a stiffly beaten egg white; dip in the flowers, hold over the batter for a moment to allow the excess to drip off, then deep-fry until golden. Drain, trim off excess stalk and serve sprinkled with sugar and a *little* chopped mint.

Squash flowers may be treated in the same way. Pick when the fruit has formed so as not to harm the plants; remove stalk and sepals. Sprinkle with sugar and pepper; serve with lemon wedges.

Walnuts are one of Dordogne's main cash crops – along with the "three Ts": tobacco, truffles and tourism. Even a single tree is a precious asset to a family, so don't get caught knocking nuts off a roadside tree, although noone will grudge you those you pick up off the tarmac – you're legitimately "rescuing" them from a squashing under the traffic.

Walnuts are used extensively for savory dishes and for alcoholic drinks, but here are a few sweet suggestions.

From eastern France, in Franche-Comté, come walnut tartlets which will be devastatingly popular with the sweet-toothed!

# Tartelettes aux Noix

### WALNUT TARTLETS
MAKES 8

pâte brisée *(see recipe)*
¾ cup *heavy cream*
1 tbsp *honey*
1½ cups *sugar*
⅛ tsp *cream of tartar*
1½ cups *quartered or roughly chopped walnuts*

Make *pâte brisée*★ as described but using 3 egg yolks; flavor with vanilla if liked. Roll out and use to line 8 deep 3 inch tartlet molds. Bake blind★ and leave to cool.

Thoroughly mix the cream and honey. Put the sugar, cream of tartar and ¾ cup water in a heavy pan and stir over a low heat until dissolved; raise heat and boil until the syrup becomes light brown. Off the heat, carefully stir in the cream mixture (it will spit violently). Return to the heat and cook to soft ball stage (240°F or when a drop of syrup forms a round ball when dripped into cold water).

Take off the heat again and stir in the walnuts; cool slightly, but spoon into tartlet shells before the filling gets too cold and stiff to handle.

# Gâteau aux Noix

### VERSATILE WALNUT CAKE
SERVES 6

1½ cups *finely crushed walnuts*
6 tbsp *flour*
¾ cup *plain sugar or vanilla sugar*
¼ cup *butter, softened*
3 *eggs*
5–6 tbsp *rum*
2 tsp *baking powder*
*vanilla (if plain sugar is used)*
*oil for greasing*

Mix the walnuts with the flour and half the sugar. Beat the butter with the remaining sugar until pale and fluffy; stir into the walnut mixture.

Beat in the eggs, one at a time, and add the rum, baking powder and vanilla. Pour the batter into an oiled and lined deep 6 inch cake pan or, 5 × 3 inch loaf pan and bake in a preheated 400°F oven for 40–45 minutes.

Serve the cake plain, buttered, frosted or with cream or icecream.

This simple walnut tart is luscious enough for a dessert; though rich and sweet, the "bite" of the nuts stops it being too much of either:

# Tarte aux Noix

### WALNUT TART
SERVES 8

Line a 12 inch flan ring or tart pan with *pâte sucrée*★ made with 2 cups flour. Prick the bottom and bake blind★ in a preheated 400°F oven for 10 minutes; remove the foil or beans and bake for a further 5–10 minutes until firm and pale gold.

Thoroughly blend 1 cup heavy cream, 1 cup sugar, 1 cup crushed walnuts, and ½ tsp vanilla. Pour into the pastry case and bake in a 275°F oven for a further 20 minutes. Leave to cool and decorate with walnut halves.

BELOW *Honeyed-caramel Walnut Tartlets and Walnut Tart*

Good tarts may also be made with almonds – here are some recipes:

# Gâteau de Pithiviers

## FLAKY ALMOND TART
SERVES 8

### The *pâte feuilletée**
3 cups *flour*
$1\frac{1}{2}$ tsp *salt*
$1\frac{1}{2}$ cups (12 oz) *butter*
$1\frac{1}{2}$ tsp *lemon juice*
about $\frac{3}{4}$ cup *iced water*

### The filling
$\frac{1}{2}$ cup *butter*
$\frac{1}{2}$ cup *sugar*
1 *egg and* 1 *yolk*
1 cup *ground almonds*
2 tbsp *flour*
2 tbsp *rum*
1 *egg beaten with* $\frac{1}{2}$ tsp *salt (for glazing)*
*granulated or confectioners' sugar*

Make the *pâte feuilletée*. Chill for 1 hour.

Cream the butter and sugar until very light and fluffy; beat in the egg and yolk. Now stir in (don't beat) the almonds, flour and rum.

Roll out almost half the pastry dough to a round about 10 inches across and set on a baking sheet; mound the filling on the center, leaving a 1 inch border all around. Brush the borders with a little of the glaze. Roll the remaining dough into a slightly thicker round, lay it over the cake as a lid and press the edges together firmly.

Scallop the edges of the tart by indenting at intervals with the back of a knife. Brush the top with the remaining glaze and, with the point of a sharp knife, score "petals" in the top: starting at the center, mark curving "spokes," each bending forward to the next (don't cut right through). Chill while the oven heats to 425°F.

Pierce a few holes around the center, sprinkle with sugar and bake for 20–25 minutes or until puffed and golden; lower the heat to 400°F and continue baking until the tart is firm, shiny on top and starting to brown. If the sugar has not melted, place it quickly under a *very* hot broiler to finish glazing. Serve at room temperature.

Almonds came to France from Italy and grow well in the southeast, near their "homeland." We got the next recipe from Aix-les-Bains in Savoy (which was an Italian kingdom, not joining France until 1860). Queen Victoria once had tea in a restaurant on the bluff above this ancient Roman spa, and condescendingly gave them her favorite recipe for scones.

# Tarte aux Amandes

## ALMOND TART
SERVES 8–10

Line a 12 inch flan ring or tart pan with *pâte brisée**; chill. Make a *crème pâtissière** using vanilla-infused milk. Mix into this $1\frac{1}{2}$ cups ground almonds, $\frac{3}{4}$ cup sugar, 3 crushed plain cookies, a pinch salt, 3 egg yolks and $\frac{1}{2}$ cup softened butter.

Spoon the mixture into the pastry case and scatter $\frac{1}{2}$ cup sliced blanched almonds on top. Bake in a preheated 400°F oven; check after 15 minutes and cover if the almonds are browning too fast. Bake for 5–10 minutes longer.

Sprinkle 2–3 tbsp rum over the top while it is still hot, and brush with a glaze made from 2 tbsp apricot jam melted with $1\frac{1}{2}$ tbsp water and strained through a sieve. Serve lukewarm.

BELOW *Almond tree in lavender field*
OPPOSITE *Flaky Almond Tart and Pignola*

# Pignola

## PINE NUT AND ALMOND TART
SERVES 6–8

pâte brisée *(see recipe)*
$\frac{1}{2}$ cup *butter, softened*
$1\frac{1}{2}$ cups *pine nuts*
$\frac{3}{4}$ cup *ground almonds*
6 tbsp *sugar (more if liked)*
3 *eggs*
$\frac{1}{4}$ cup *potato starch or cornstarch*
$\frac{1}{2}$ tsp *baking powder*
*pinch salt*

Make *pâte brisée** using $2\frac{1}{4}$ cups flour and 4 egg yolks; flavor it with a few drops of vanilla. Chill, roll out and line an 11 inch flan ring or tart pan.

Heat a quarter of the butter and lightly brown the pine nuts, stirring carefully over a medium heat.

Mix the ground almonds and sugar in a bowl; beat in the eggs one by one, beating until very light. Mix together the potato starch, baking powder and salt. Sift over the mixture and fold in very lightly, adding the remaining melted butter just before the end.

Pour into the pastry case and bake in a preheated 375°F oven for 10–12 minutes. Remove from the oven and very quickly spread the pine nuts over the surface in one even layer; return and bake for 18–20 minutes longer. The pastry should be light brown with a firm filling; turn the oven down if it browns too fast. Cool on a wire rack.

ABOVE *Galette Bressane, traditionally accompanied by cream, cream cheese or fruit*

At the *auberges*, the wayside houses where a traveler could find a bed for the night, the woman of the house came to realize that her lodgers would also appreciate a meal, and she began to lay places for them at the family supper table. Thus was born the *table d'hôte*, and for many years all *auberge* cooking was done by women. This *cuisine des mères* tradition has lasted and many famous restaurants still serve some traditional *auberge* dishes. Here's one:

# Galette Bressane

## BAKED "PANCAKE"
SERVES 4–6

1 *cake* (0.6 oz) *compressed yeast or* 2 tsp
  *active dry yeast*
*sugar* (*see recipe*)
1¾ cups *flour*
*pinch salt*
1 cup (½ lb) *butter*
1 *egg*
*grated rind of lemon*
2 tbsp *Grand Marnier* (*or other fruit
  liqueur*), *rum or orange-flower water*

Mash the yeast with 1 tsp sugar in 3 tbsp warm water and leave in a warm place to froth up. Sift the flour and salt into a bowl; soften two-thirds of the butter.

Make a well in the flour and pour in the yeast mixture; gradually add the softened butter, egg, lemon rind, flavoring and 1–2 tbsp sugar if you have a sweet tooth, working with your hand to make a soft but not runny dough. (If necessary, add a little more flour or lukewarm water.) Leave in a fairly cool place for 1 hour; the dough will rise slightly and become more manageable.

Knead lightly and roll out as thinly as possible (1/10 inch); if it is easier, divide in half first. Transfer to greased baking sheet(s), flake the remaining butter over the surface and sprinkle with up to ¼ cup sugar; bake in a preheated 450°F oven for 5–8 minutes. Then *either* turn up the oven to hottest and bake the *galette* on the top shelf for 3 more minutes *or* cook it under the hottest possible broiler, turning it around as each section browns, to caramelize the top. Serve in wedges, plain or with cream, cream cheese or fruit salad.

There's a tradition of recipes originating from convents in France. One of the most famous is:

# Macarons

## ALMOND MACAROONS
MAKES ABOUT 16

Grind (not too finely) 2 cups blanched almonds (or use 1½ cups ready-ground almonds) and mix with ¾ cups of sugar. Beat 2 small egg whites until lightly frothy but not stiff. Stir into the mixture, a little at a time, adding a few drops of vanilla, stop as soon as mixture binds into a stiff paste (you may not need all the egg white). Place silicone or rice paper on a baking sheet and drop round blobs of the mixture onto it, flattening slightly; sprinkle with sugar and bake in a preheated 400°F oven. Cooking time is about 18–20 minutes, but check after 16; macaroons should be crisp and golden outside, softer and chewy within. Cool on rack (remove carefully from silicone paper with a spatula first). Delicious macaroons can also be made using walnuts or hazelnuts.

Almond macaroons are often credited to the convent at Nancy in Lorraine, whose nuns (like so many others) "went commercial" after the Revolution; the Sœurs Macarons bakery still exists there. But the claims of the nuns of St Emilion can't be ignored, especially as *charlottes* (see p. 80) made with macaroons instead of ladyfingers are known as "St Emilions." Another convent with a reputation for sweet cooking was that of Baume-les-Dames in Franche-Comté: its postulants had to be of noble ancestry unto the fourth generation and it's associated with crisp little fritters known as *pets de nonne*.

They are simply teaspoon-sized blobs of *pâte à choux*★ flavored with grated lemon rind and a little orange-flower water, and deep fried until crisp.

The next cake is also in the *"mère"* tradition and comes from Normandy:

# Gâteau aux Pommes

## NORMAN APPLE CAKE
SERVES 8–10

5–6 *apples*
3 *eggs*
1 cup *sugar*
¾ cup *butter, melted*
2 cups *flour*
2 tsp *baking powder*
*pinch salt*
5 tbsp *Calvados ( or rum )*
*melted butter*
*sugar for sprinkling*

Peel and core apples; cut 2 into rings, slice the remainder. Beat the eggs with the sugar until pale and thick; pour in the butter and beat again. Sift in the flour, baking powder and salt; continue beating until smooth. Stir in the spirit and the sliced apples.

Line an 8 × 10 inch baking pan with greased parchment paper; lay the apple rings on the bottom and pour the batter over. Brush with a little melted butter and bake in a preheated 375°F oven for 1 hour or until well risen and firm. Unmold onto a serving plate and sprinkle liberally with sugar; eat warm. (Served hot, with cream or custard, it makes a popular family dessert.)

BELOW *Normandy cider apples waiting to be pressed*

Many French families concoct their own cheese spreads; once these were made from their own "home-grown" milk, but many traditional mixtures are just as easy to make with town-bought ingredients. One such is *cervelle de canut*. *Canuts* were the weavers who made Lyon a world leader in the silk industry; *cervelle* means "brain" and I can only assume that it refers to the domed shape of the cheese when it's turned out of its bowl. (If this name puts you off, call it by its other one – *claqueret lyonnais*.)

Into ½ pound (1 cup) cream (or cottage) cheese, beat 1 tbsp each chopped parsley and chives, 1 *finely*-chopped garlic clove, a small minced shallot, salt and pepper. Then add 2–3 tbsp *crème fraîche*★, 5 tbsp dry white wine and 1 tbsp oil; beat again and taste for seasoning. If to use the

BELOW *Throughout France sheep are accompanied all day to prevent them straying*

same day, press tightly into a bowl and chill before turning out onto a plate. Otherwise pack into a round strainer to drain; turn out later.

Spread on bread, toast, crackers or – as country families used to do – serve with hot baked or boiled potatoes.

One of our childhood breakfast favourites used to be "French toast." In France it's known as *pain perdu* ("lost bread" – presumably bread which would otherwise be lost because it's stale), or *daudines* (a Périgord name whose meaning I can't trace) or – most descriptively – *pain des pauvres* (paupers' bread). Unlike my version, it is always sweet in France and served with jam, currant jelly or honey.

In case anyone doesn't know it: soak slices of stale bread very briefly in milk (with sugar and vanilla if liked) then pull slowly through beaten egg; fry in a little very hot fat until the outside is crisp and brown.

Fancy breads always make a welcome change. To make *Pain aux Prunes* (Plum Bread) from the Dordogne: take some ordinary white bread dough – your baker may sell it, or there's a recipe (*pâte à pain*) on p. 138 – and knead into it 2 tbsp slightly softened fat (the Périgordians prefer goose fat but any sort will do). Roll it out to about 1 inch thick and spread with prepared fruit, adding sugar if necessary (see next paragraph), leaving wide borders all around. Roll up and seal edges well before baking on an oiled and floured baking sheet – 45–50 minutes in a preheated 400°F oven, or until loaf sounds hollow when tapped.

Cooking makes the fruit juices run. If fruit is *very* sweet, such as apricots, cherries or some types of plum, you should need no sugar; *firm* plums such as greengages, or apples, may be sprinkled with sugar before rolling up. (Remove any pits before cooking.) Cut the bread in thick slices to serve.

ABOVE *Unusual French varieties of home-baked bread: Plum Bread (left) and Onion and Walnut Bread*

# Pain aux Oignons et aux Noix

## ONION AND WALNUT BREAD
MAKES 2 LOAVES

1½ cups *finely chopped onion*
6 tbsp *walnut (or other) oil*
1 *cake* (0.6 oz) *compressed yeast or* 2 tsp
    *active dry yeast*
1 tsp *sugar*
2 cups *lukewarm water*
1 tbsp *salt*
6¼ cups *bread or all-purpose flour*
1½ cups *roughly chopped walnuts*
*melted butter for greasing*
*egg for glazing*

Fry the onions gently in oil until cooked and starting to brown. Mix the yeast and sugar with a third of the water, stir well and leave in a warm place to froth up. Mix the salt, chopped onion and walnut oil with the remaining water.

Sift the flour into a large bowl, make a well and add the frothy yeast mixture. Mix in with your hand, adding the onion mixture a little at a time, until you have a soft but not sloppy dough. (Different temperatures and flours require more or less liquid; add more plain warm water or flour if necessary.)

Knead for 5–10 minutes until smooth and elastic.

Roll the dough into a ball and leave – either in the bowl covered with a cloth, or in an oiled plastic bag – in a warm place to double in size (about 1–1½ hours).

Meanwhile generously butter 2 pans (5 × 3 inch loaf, deep 7 inch cake, or small savarin molds).

Punch down the dough and knead again, this time incorporating the chopped nuts. Divide in half, shape as appropriate and put into the pans; leave in a warm place for 30 minutes longer.

Slash the tops with a sharp knife or make scissor snips, glaze with beaten egg and bake in a preheated 425°F oven for 10–15 minutes; lower heat to 375°F and bake for 30–40 minutes longer, or until the loaves sound hollow when tapped (a ring mold may cook faster than a loaf pan, a round one more slowly). Remove the loaves, invert them in their pans and replace in the oven for 5 minutes to harden the undersides. Cool slowly.

Excellent fresh or, later, toasted – with cheese or butter.

# Nourriture des Champs et des Bois

## FOOD FROM FIELD AND FOREST

Thrift being a quality innate to the French country wife, she lost no opportunity to find food that was free. To this end she (or her mother-in-law) made frequent forays for wild fruits, leaves, flowers and fungi which could be put to good use. The habit persists today: middle-aged women are often seen quartering the meadows armed with a basket and a well-worn sharp knife; weekend family outings scour the woods for mushrooms; grandmothers scuttle out after autumn gales to gather fallen chestnuts.

Dandelion leaves are excellent in salads. Pick them young before flowering – best from February to April; don't use those alongside main roads – they may be lead-polluted.

The photograph (below) shows an appetizer based on dandelions. It is made of diced *sauté* potatoes, cubes of bread fried in garlic butter, cooked shelled shrimp (leave a few unshelled for decoration), strips of fried bacon – all in whatever proportions you fancy. Mix well with prepared dandelion leaves and, if liked, some broken spears of Belgian endive. Toss in a garlicky vinaigrette★ and serve immediately.

Simpler salads have been prepared for centuries. For example:

# Salade aux Pissenlits

## DANDELION AND POTATO SALAD
SERVES 6

Cook 2½ lbs peeled and roughly chopped potatoes in boiling salted water until just tender, 15–20 minutes. Drain. Meanwhile heat 2 tbsp pork drippings or bacon fat, into which put 2 double handfuls well-washed dandelion leaves. Add salt, pepper and about ½ cup wine vinegar; stir over a medium heat for about 10 minutes until the leaves start to soften. Toss with the potatoes and serve very hot.

# Pissenlits au Lard

## DANDELIONS WITH BACON
SERVES 6

Fry ½ cup diced slab bacon until crisp; pick out with slotted spoon and keep hot. Pour ½ cup wine (or cider) vinegar into pan, add black pepper and *déglacer* thoroughly.

Put three double handfuls of washed, trimmed dandelion leaves into a well-heated serving bowl and add the bacon bits and the pan mixture. Mix quickly and serve at once.

An English friend of ours living in France horrified visiting friends and relations: acquiring a taste for dandelion dishes, she actually bought seed to grow her own . . .

BELOW *An exotic dandelion and shrimp appetizer; see recipe left*

Spring also brings on that other arch-enemy of the garden – nettles. They make a lovely soup.

# Soupe aux Orties

## NETTLE SOUP

½ lb *young nettle leaves ( or spinach or watercress)*
3 tbsp *butter*
2 tbsp *oil*
2–3 *leeks, sliced ( or 1–2 Spanish onions, chopped)*
1 lb *potatoes, peeled and chopped roughly ( about 3 cups)*
*salt and pepper*
¾ cup *heavy cream,* crème fraîche★ *or sour cream*

Wash the nettles and remove any stalks (wear gloves). Melt the butter and oil in a large pan, stir in the leeks and nettles and cook gently until they start to soften. Add the potatoes and 1 quart water; season and leave to simmer steadily for 25–40 minutes.

Mill or liquidize the soup, check seasoning and reheat, adding more water or stock if too thick; pour the cream into a warmed tureen, pour on the soup, stir and serve. Or pour the soup into individual bowls stirring in a little cream afterwards. Good hot or cold.

The subject of herbs – for restorative *tisanes* and cold drinks, as medicines, or in cooking – is much too extensive to be dealt with here. But perhaps I might just mention that mint not only makes a pleasing "tea" that is thought good for headaches; it makes a refreshing cooling summer drink, too.

Just put 10–12 leaves (any type – mixed varieties if you like) in a bottle of cold (ideally spring) water and store in the refrigerator for 48 hours. Sweeten only if you must.

RIGHT *Nettle Soup is easy and inexpensive to prepare, but the leaves must be young*

ABOVE *Blackberry Jelly. The French love to serve jams on baked or boiled potatoes*

Wild fruits were important of course. Naturally you MUST NOT EAT ivy, mistletoe, privet hedge, honeysuckle, deadly nightshade (belladonna), yew, etc. Thrushes love holly, and they make holly *eau-de-vie* in Alsace, but you should shun it. French grannies used hawthorn berries (*after* the frost), but I was taught to leave them alone and don't recommend them. If in doubt, don't pick.

But there's still plenty to choose from. Like us, the French love blackberries. They still reckon them good for sore throats – even an infusion of blackberry leaves is considered effective.

# Confiture aux Mûres

## BLACKBERRY JELLY

Stir fruit over low heat, crushing to release all juice. When almost boiling, strain and squeeze through a cloth; measure juice. Dissolve with 1 cup sugar per 2½ cups juice and boil until jelly tests done. Skim, pour and seal.

Countryfolk adore this jam on potatoes (see photograph above) and it *is* extraordinarily good. To go sinfully over the top, by all means add butter too!

*Confiture de Baies de Sureau* (Elderberry Jelly) is made as above but add more sugar – 1½ cups per 2½ cups of juice. For *Confiture de Myrtilles* (Blueberry Jelly) add sugar as for elderberry.

**Important** If you want your jelly clear, do *not* squeeze it but leave to strain through a jelly bag.

# Confiture des Baies de Rosier

## ROSE HIP JELLY

Leave the hips, garden or wild, until after the first frosts; when they start to wither they will be softer and sweeter.

Top and tail washed berries and put in a kettle with a little water to stop them sticking. Bring to a boil, then simmer without stirring till very soft (45–60 minutes).

Sieve (the seeds of some *wild* rosehips contain an irritant, so be quite sure to strain them all out). Put into a clean pan, with a little boiling water if the pulp is very thick. Cook gently for 10–15 minutes longer; strain through a cloth.

Measure this juice and add 1¼ cups sugar per 2½ cups juice. Stir to dissolve; cook for 20 minutes, add grated lemon rind (approx. ½ lemon per 2½ cups) and cook for 10 minutes longer. Pour and seal.

The European mountain ash or rowan tree has the delightful name of *sorbier des oiseaux* in French. As in English folklore, it is supposed to be a great protector against evil.

The berries are best after the first frost; one must compromise between this perfection and the possible loss to birds if one leaves them too long!

# Confiture aux Sorbiers

## ROWAN OR MULBERRY JELLY

Wash the berries and strip them from their stalks with a fork; measure. Wash and roughly chop an equal quantity of crab apples or tart apples (no need to peel or core) and put all together in a large kettle with the juice and sliced peel of 1 lemon per 4 pints fruit. Add a little water, almost to cover; bring to a boil and simmer until really soft (time varies greatly – check after 40 minutes). Strain overnight through a jelly bag; do not squeeze.

Measure the juice. Warm 2 cups sugar per 2½ cups juice and add it to the reheated juice; stir over medium heat until it dissolves. Boil until jelly tests done (10–12 minutes), then skim, pour and seal.

Marvelous with game and other hot or cold meats.

Fruit paste is still popular in many areas as a sweetmeat. Using as little water as possible, the fruit is sieved to a thick pulp before adding sugar; instead of using glasses, it is left to set in shallow containers, then cut up to eat with the fingers.

# Pâte de Coings

## QUINCE PASTE

Wash and quarter the fruit. Don't bother to peel or core, but cut away any hardened vestiges of stem or flower and any bad bits. Put in a kettle with a very little water. Cover, bring to a boil and simmer until just tender (start checking after 10 minutes – times will vary); drain well.

Push through a food mill or coarse sieve; measure the purée. Stir in an equal quantity of sugar over low heat. Bring to a boil, then simmer gently, stirring to prevent sticking, for a further 10 minutes.

Pour into plates, bowls, saucers or other shallow containers and leave for several days, protected from insects, until really set and hardened. Cut into fingers.

For a more refined *pâte*, suitable for boxing as a gift, proceed as before, but sieve finely. If liked, add a little flavoring with the sugar (eg. a few drops of vanilla). After cooling, cut the set paste into squares or small dominoes and press into sugar to coat on all sides; leave for a day or two longer under a mesh in an airy place to become firm before further handling.

Treat apples, crab apples, pears, japonica fruit or medlars in exactly the same way. For soft fruits and plums, cherries, apricots etc. the method is slightly different: adapt a favorite Plum Butter recipe. (A *little* cinnamon is nice with plums and cherries; cook a cinnamon stick with the fruit – remembering to remove it before milling.)

BELOW *Elderberry Jelly on bread; Rosehip Jelly on gaudes (cornmeal porridge); Rowan Jelly; Quince and Sloe Pastes*

RIGHT *Chestnut Soup, a tasty combination of chestnuts, beans and oranges*

Autumn has always meant chestnuts, freely available even today from communal woods. Where cereals could not be grown, chestnuts provided for centuries the only "flour" for many people and was even used to make bread. (Chestnut flour is still used largely in several Corsican specialties.) To peel chestnuts, see p. 140.

Chestnut soups, some exceedingly simple, are popular in many regions. A good one comes from Brittany. The old version was rather bland, bulked out with potatoes and cream; here is a variation adapted to suit modern tastes:

# Soupe aux Marrons

## CHESTNUT SOUP
SERVES 6–8

1–1¼ lbs *peeled chestnuts, or drained canned*
1 *carrot, chopped roughly*
1 *leek, chopped*
1 *small turnip, chopped roughly*
⅔ cup *dried navy beans, soaked overnight in unsalted water and drained*
1 *onion, peeled and chopped roughly*
*salt and pepper*
½ cup *diced slab bacon*
3 quarts *chicken stock*★
*juice of 1–2 oranges*
*finely shredded orange rind (optional)*
*chopped chervil or parsley for garnish (optional)*

Put all the ingredients except the orange juice, rind and herbs in a large saucepan and cook gently for 1½ hours. Mill finely or liquidize. The soup should be quite thick; if it is not, simmer gently, uncovered, until it reaches the required consistency.

Reheat before serving, stir in the orange juice and, if liked, sprinkle with the shredded rind and chopped chervil or parsley.

RIGHT *Chestnut Pudding*

Chestnut sauce★ is a classic accompaniment for furred game, especially venison; it's also good with lamb, turkey or guinea fowl.

The oldest and simplest chestnut recipe we know is *Châtaignes Blanchies* (Steamed Chestnuts). Roughly chop a few washed potatoes and lay thickly in the bottom of a well-greased heavy pan or flameproof casserole. Almost fill with peeled chestnuts and cover (ideally, seal the lid on with flour-and-water paste). Cook on a medium heat until it starts to sing, then lower heat and cook for 20–30 minutes; discard the potatoes. The chestnuts will have cooked in their own and the potatoes' steam.

Floury and slightly sweetish, they're an unusual substitute for potatoes to partner braised meat or game (photograph, opposite). Save any which become slightly scorched to eat as sweet "nibbles."

Finally, a luscious chestnut dessert:

# Gâteau aux Châtaignes

## CHESTNUT PUDDING
SERVES 10–12

¾ lb *peeled chestnuts or drained canned*
4 *squares ( 1 oz each ) semisweet*
    *chocolate*
¾ cup *butter, melted*
4 *eggs ( 2 whole, 2 separated )*
½ cup *sugar or to taste*
*milk ( see recipe )*
*vanilla*

Simmer peeled chestnuts★ in boiling water until fairly tender; drain and mill or liquidize. (If using a processor, stop short of absolute smoothness.)

Meanwhile, melt the broken-up chocolate in 2 tbsp butter and stir until smooth. If using canned purée, heat gently until it pops, to dry it slightly. Into the still-hot purée beat the remaining butter, whole eggs and yolks, chocolate and sugar. Add just enough milk to make a stiffish purée (probably unnecessary with canned purée). Fold in the stiffly beaten egg whites and flavor with a few drops of vanilla (unless you are using vanilla sugar).

Butter a large loaf pan or metal terrine – about 10 × 5 inches – and

*ABOVE Steamed chestnuts ( châtaignes blanchies ) served with braised guinea fowl*

spoon in the mixture, leaving a good ½ inch space at the top. Cover with foil and set in a pan of boiling water; cook in a preheated 300°F oven for 40 minutes, a little longer if using canned purée. Turn off oven and leave to cool. Chill thoroughly before unmolding.

Decorate with whipped cream, or hand cream separately.

**Note** This can be made with unsweetened canned chestnut purée, but preparing your own gives a pleasant, less bland, texture.

OPPOSITE *Mushroom Soup*
ABOVE *Sniffing a freshly-dug truffle is the best way to gauge its quality and value*

Any visitor to France will be aware of the huge range of fungi which appear on French tables and, except for the *champignon de Paris* (button mushroom), they are nearly all wild. American varieties are slightly fewer but just as useful. It is well worth buying one of the excellent books on the subject, but be sure to read carefully before you go gathering; eat *nothing* until you are *one hundred percent certain* of its safety.

Most wild mushrooms are tasty enough to be eaten alone, lightly fried in butter, or with a fine sprinkling of chopped parsley and garlic in the French manner.

They may be preserved in many ways. Sealed in canning jars in brine, or chopped and lightly sweated in a *very* little butter or oil, then frozen. They dry splendidly: thread on strings and hang in a warm, dry place; soak in water or stock to plump out again when needed. I find them unsuitable for simply frying at this stage, but they're excellent for all other uses.

This is a rather rich soup recipe. If you like the taste of parsley, don't remove it where instructed – but chop it beforehand:

# Potage aux Meuniers

## MUSHROOM SOUP

*Meuniers* are little wild mushrooms, plentiful in Normandy; you can substitute young fresh field mushrooms (before the gills turn brown) or button ones.

1¼ cups *ground or finely chopped cooked chicken*
1 tbsp *Calvados or other brandy*
6 tbsp *butter*
¼ cup *flour*
1 quart *milk*
*grated nutmeg*
3½ cups *finely chopped mushrooms*
3 tbsp *lemon juice*
2 *parsley sprigs*
*salt and pepper*
2 *egg yolks*
½ cup *heavy cream*

Leave the chicken to soak with the Calvados. Make a cream sauce with a third of the butter, the flour and half the milk; flavor with nutmeg.

Put the mushrooms in a frying pan with the remaining butter, lemon juice and parsley. Stir over a medium heat until the mushrooms release their juice. Remove parsley and season; combine with the sauce and the chicken, plus its marinade. Pour in the rest of the milk, stir until combined and simmer very gently for 15 minutes.

Beat the egg yolks into the cream. Remove the soup from the heat and slowly pour in the egg and cream liaison, stirring very briskly to thicken slightly without curdling. (The soup is meant to be very thick and creamy; if you find it too much so, dilute with more hot milk and adjust the seasoning if necessary.) Serve.

Of course the finest and most famous fungi of all are truffles. Free to those who know where to look, they are shatteringly expensive to buy. This is why I don't propose to discuss their uses in cooking here – even though their pervasive flavor means a little truffle, luckily, goes a very long way.

# Confits, Confitures et Boissons

## PRESERVES (SAVORY AND SWEET) AND DRINKS

Very characteristic of the French country kitchen was its pantry. Busy as she was, the housewife nevertheless *had* to find time to can, salt, pickle or otherwise preserve every scrap of surplus food in season. She couldn't afford waste and, more important, without cans or commercially bottled items, this was her only means of bringing variety to the family's off-season diet.

*Confire* means to preserve or pickle – from which comes *confiture* (jam); but the most important and exciting of all *confits* was meat.

In the coldest part of winter, every family killed a pig. Neighbors came in to help with the enormous labor of salting and curing hams, bacon and *petit salé*★, making blood sausages and other sausages, and preparing *fromage de tête* (head cheese). In between all this, time was found to cook meals for the helpers, and hard work meant huge appetites! Ears, feet and skin might have been preserved to provide superbly flavored additions to future soups and bean stews.

Most modern *confits* are made from ducks and geese which have been *gavé* (specially fattened) for *foie gras*, and the preserved pieces are served as a delicacy in their own right as well as to impart their special savor to soups. (The breasts of such birds, known as *magrets*, are even more prized and are cooked fresh in butter like extra-succulent steaks.)

Any sort of meat may be *confit*; poultry, rabbits and cheap – but lean – cuts of pork are best. In addition you'll need plenty of *gros sel* (coarse or sea salt), crushed black peppercorns, garlic, bay leaves, thyme or other herbs and masses of extra fat, preferably "matching" the meat (use pork or chicken fat for rabbit).

LEFT *Preserved Duck accompanied by Tomates Provençales (recipe p. 79)*

LEFT *Duck pieces and bundles of pork skin on a bed of salt, pepper and herbs, ready to be confit*

*To serve* **Confit de Canard**
(*Preserved Duck*)
Very slowly melt the fat from 4 pieces of *canard confit* (see above) and allow to heat through. Pour off fat, turn up heat and brown pieces until the skin is deliciously crisp. Serve with potatoes, mushrooms and *tomates provençales* (photograph opposite) or with green peas and snipped bacon.

Nothing was (nor is) wasted from the pig; even the skin was preserved. And even if you've no need for such economy, you'll appreciate this as an unusual way of adding instant flavor to soups, stews, lentil and other meatless dishes:

# Confit (d'Oie, de Canard, de Lapin, de Porc)

## PRESERVED GOOSE, DUCK, RABBIT, PORK

Cut up ducks into four portions – geese into up to eight – leaving the main carcass, neck and end pieces for stock; cut up rabbits into five; divide other meats into equivalent portions (your butcher should do this for you on request). Cut slanting slits in the meat and insert thin slivers of garlic (if slits go straight inwards, garlic may fall out in cooking). Now rub all over generously with salt, pepper and crumbled chosen herbs. Put pieces in a large bowl with a little more salt and leave in a cool place for 6–12 hours according to the thickness of the meat. Small pieces will be "flavored" in 6 hours or less, really big ones may take 24 hours or more (but too long a wait leads to oversalting).

Melt plenty of fat slowly in readiness. Wipe the pieces and lay them in a wide pan; cover completely with melted fat and cook in a very cool oven (about 175°F) so that the fat barely moves. Traditionally the confit is cooked when a straw penetrates easily, which may take up to 1½ hours, but test small or thin pieces with a fine skewer after 20–25 minutes: any juice which shows from a skewer prick should be colorless. (As the meat is to be kept, it *must* be cooked, but overcooking makes it unpalatably dry.)

Pack the pieces either in a large earthenware crock or, one or two at a time, in canning jars. Strain the fat through a fine cloth and reheat in a clean pan until bubbles cease – indicating that all moisture has gone. Cool slightly, then pour over meat. Tap jars gently but firmly to dislodge all traces of air, and add more fat as necessary to cover the meat generously.

When set, check for airholes (add more fat if need be), scatter with salt and seal. Leave at least a week before use; it will keep several months in a cool cellar, indefinitely in the refrigerator – but don't freeze.

To use, dig out the pieces you need, melt the fat off them slowly and use it to reseal the pot. (The fat may be re-used once or twice but eventually becomes too salty.) Use the meat to flavor *cassoulets*, *garbures* or other vegetable soups, or serve it as a main course (see next recipe).

# Couennes Confites

## PRESERVED PORK SKIN

Remove the skin from a roast, or buy it separately. Cut or scrape away most of the inside fat, and melt this with more pork (or bacon) fat. Cut the skin into 1 inch wide strips and rub with sea salt and seasonings, as described for making *confit*. Leave in a bowl, weighted, overnight.

Wipe off excess salt and seasonings. Press 3–4 strips of skin together, fold into 2 or 3 and tie firmly into bundles. When all the skin is tied, cook as for *confit*, but for longer: perhaps 2 hours. Check tenderness with needle or fine skewer.

Pack 2–3 bundles at a time into canning jars, not too tightly. Put the fat in to one-third depth and leave to set before filling to cover (otherwise the bundles will float); cover and store as for *confit*. Use exactly as you would meat *confits* for flavoring. The skin can also be cut up into small pieces, fried crisp and eaten on its own as party nibbles. Bundles of 6–8 strips of rind saved from the breakfast bacon can be treated in the same way, but need salting for a shorter time.

We all know about making jam from everyday fruits; *grand'mère* used a wider range of unexpected ingredients.

# Marmelade de Potiron au Citron

### PUMPKIN JAM WITH LEMON

4–4½ lbs *pumpkin*
3–4 *lemons*
8–8½ cups *sugar*

Peel and de-seed pumpkin and cut into fairly small pieces. Scrub the lemons and cut in 2 or 4 lengthwise; remove seeds (tie these in a small cheesecloth bag to help setting later). Cut into *paper-thin* slices (otherwise the rind will be tough).

In a large bowl, jar or crock, layer the pumpkin pieces with the sugar and lemon slivers. Leave to soak overnight.

Pour the fruit and juices into a kettle; add the seed bag, tied to the pan with a string, and heat very slowly, stirring often until the mixture boils. Cook steadily, watching that it does not burn, until a spoonful of juice will set on a cold plate – about 30–40 minutes. Skim, remove seeds and cool slightly, then pour into warm jars and seal. Process in boiling water before storage.

# Marmelade de Potiron et de Poires

### PUMPKIN AND PEAR JAM

Make this exactly as above, but up to half the weight of pumpkin may be replaced with peeled, cored and quartered (or sliced) pears.

If you have lots of pears but no pumpkin, you can make jam of them in much the same way. Use only half the quantity of sugar to fruit, soak for a few hours as above, adding the juice and grated rind of at least 1 lemon plus 1 tbsp white wine vinegar per 4 lbs pears. During cooking add a vanilla bean split lengthwise (remove it before pouring).

BELOW *Ripe pumpkins on sale in an autumn market*

# Confiture de Tomates Vertes

### GREEN TOMATO JAM

**Note** My old recipe uses 1 lemon for this quantity of fruit; I find 2 or 3 an improvement.

6 lbs *firm green tomatoes*
8 cups *sugar, or a little more*
*lemons (see note above), sliced paper thin*

Wash, wipe and slice the tomatoes crosswise. Layer them with the sugar and lemon slices in a preserving kettle; leave for 24 hours.

Heat very slowly, stirring gently from time to time until it boils; then cook gently until the jam becomes a pretty amber color and a spoonful of juice sets in a cold saucer. Skim, pour into warm jars and seal. Process in a boiling water bath before storage.

Gorgeous with *fromage frais* or cream cheese, sprinkled with lemon juice.

RIGHT *Pumpkin and Pear Jam (left) and Pumpkin Jam with Lemon*

My family used to make what we called Old Boys' Jam; in France it's *Confiture d'Officiers* and it could hardly be simpler.

As each fruit comes into season, put some, together with its weight in sugar, in layers in a large, wide-mouthed jar, then carefully pour in any white alcohol (gin, *marc*, vodka, *eau-de-vie* or one of those strange spirits you bought on vacation) just to cover. Try to alternate colors, e.g. cherries, apricots, raspberries, peaches. Don't use bananas, pineapples, strawberries (they go brown) or citrus fruits. Cork tightly and keep in a cool place between additions. (Pit cherries; halve and pit apricots and plums; quarter or slice peaches. Make sure the final layer is well covered with spirit.)

Don't try to save it for longer than three or four months if you want it to keep its color and freshness. Hardly a jam for breakfast, but delicious for raising plain ice cream to dinner-party status.

A *dégustation* of fruit in alcohol is as commonly offered as a cup of coffee to visitors in French country houses. Cherries, plums and prunes are the most-often-used fruit for this delicacy. (Even today, many households have the legal right to their own spirits – made from fruit, or *marc* from their wine presses. These are taken, if there's no local distillery, to an itinerant distiller – *bouilleur du cru* – who travels the neighborhood in season, setting up his still on suitable sites. Alas, times change: bureaucracy is abolishing this agreeable practice.)

LEFT *Officer's Jam*   BELOW *An itinerant distiller, still a fairly common sight in rural France*

# Pruneaux au Vin

### PRUNES IN WINE
(Sometimes called *Agenais au Château*)

Prick 1¼ lbs (about 3 cups) prunes all over with a darning needle and pack them loosely in canning jars to about three quarters full. Into a pan put *either* 2 vanilla beans, up to 1 cup brandy or rum, ⅔ cup sugar (or to taste) and a bottle of red wine *or* a ¾ tsp powdered cinnamon and a bottle of sweet white wine. Bring to a boil and pour over the prunes, to cover; add more liquor as prunes swell. When cool prick out any air bubbles. Seal – and try to wait at least a month before opening (the longer you can wait, the better it is likely to taste!).

Serve one prune and a little of the liquid in a liqueur glass or tiny bowl for each guest, who nibbles at the fruit with a teaspoon and finishes by drinking the wine.

For a headier mixture, infuse 2 lbs (about 5 cups) prunes in hot tea for 24 hours; drain. Make a syrup by dissolving 5 tbsp white sugar in a little water; bring to a boil then mix with a bottle of Armagnac or other brandy. Pour over the prunes in jars and seal as above.

*Pickled prunes* are also pleasing to eat and child's play to make. Soak and simmer to plumpness the required number of prunes. Drain and pack loosely into canning jars, adding a very small chili pepper (or half a large one) and 10 coriander seeds to each jar. Cover with (preferably sherry) vinegar, tapping to exclude all air bubbles. Seal and leave for at least 2 weeks before use.

If you have a peach tree – never mind if it rarely or never produces fruit – pick some of the tender young leaves towards the end of spring and delight your friends, as the advertisements say, with one of these delectable drinks.

# Apéritif aux Feuilles de Pêcher

### PEACH-LEAF APERITIF

(Other fragrant leaves – black currant, verbena, lemon-geranium – may be substituted.)

60 *peach leaves (or other leaf, see above)*
1 *bottle white (or red) wine (see* **Note** *opposite)*
4 *cloves*
½ *cinnamon stick*
½ cup *sugar, or to taste*
½ cup *eau-de-vie or spirit (as p. 113).*

Soak the leaves in the wine and spices for a week. Strain; add the sugar and spirit, stirring well to dissolve the sugar; bottle. Not much patience needed: it's ready to drink after another week!

# Vin de Feuilles de Pêcher

## PEACH-LEAF WINE

(Again, other fragrant leaves can be used; see above.)

60 *peach leaves*
1 quart *red (or white) wine (see* **Note** *below)*
2 *drops vanilla*
1 tbsp *coriander seeds*
*small piece of cinnamon stick*
3 *small apples, quartered*

Macerate together for 30 days. Filter, bottle, and store in a cool place.

**Note** Great vintage wines would be wasted for these recipes, but don't use anything you find nasty in its plain state either. If you use leftovers from a party, do so within 24 hours.

OPPOSITE *Walnut Liqueur (left) and Pickled Prunes*

Perhaps you've enjoyed that intriguing walnut liqueur that they sell throughout Dordogne and Périgord. Provided you can lay hands on soft green walnuts, picked around the end of June, you can make some yourself. There are many recipes; here's one:

# Brou de Noix

## WALNUT LIQUER

Halve 50 green walnuts; remove any cores, then crush into a pulp and put in a large, wide-mouthed sealable jar. Mix 2 lightly-crushed mint leaves (*or a blade of mace and the finely pared rind of a lemon*), 5–6 cloves and a piece of cinnamon stick with 3 cups *eau-de-vie* or spirit (as p. 113). Pour over nut pulp; cover and soak for 30 days in a warm place.

Strain through jelly bag, squeezing to extract all juice. Measure the liquid and add $\frac{1}{3}$–$\frac{1}{2}$ cup sugar per $2\frac{1}{2}$ cups liquid. Stir well, re-seal and leave 10 days longer, shaking occasionally to dissolve the sugar. Strain, filter (coffee filter papers are ideal) and bottle: it's now ready to drink.

*Pickled walnuts* are a well-known English favorite. If you'd like a variation of this delicacy (and perhaps have nimble-fingered children seeking a wet day's occupation), try the old French version.

Shell 2 lbs walnuts. Boil a little white vinegar – about $1\frac{1}{2}$ inches in a smallish pan – and throw in some of the nuts. Wearing rubber gloves to prevent staining your fingers, remove a few at a time and peel off the brown skins (see peeling chestnuts★). Put the peeled nuts into canning jars, together with 10–20 black peppercorns and a sprig of tarragon; fill with fresh white vinegar to cover – you will need about 1 quart, but this depends on your jar(s). Seal. Good with cold meats after a week.

In days gone by, when home remedies were commonplace, there was considerable interest in medicines for longevity. An old Provençal nostrum, dating from before the Middle Ages, was administered – together with suitable prayers – against plague, cholera and smallpox. It was (and perhaps still is) considered good for "heart-ache," fevers, gout, indigestion, toothache and constipation. Made by infusing aloes, gentian, agaric, saffron, rhubarb, quinine, senna, juniper and veronica root (among other things) in a mixture of wine and *eau-de-vie*, it is said to "cheer up and enliven old people, keeping them strong and gay" – which, no doubt, is why its name is *Elixir de Longue Vie*.

Another ancient rejuvenator, particularly popular in the Auvergne, is *eau-de-vie de vipère*. (I had always thought that those snakes in bottles in the windows of homeopathic druggists in France were specimens helpfully displayed for snake-identification; perhaps they're really this miraculous cure-all?) I have a sixteenth-century recipe for viper brandy, not without its perils, in which you catch an adder by the tail and then ... but perhaps you'd rather not hear about that?

LEFT *Ripe cherries may be made into jam, liqueur (Kirsch), used in desserts (see Clafoutis aux Cerises, p. 89), or, best of all, simply eaten raw*

# Casse-Croûtes, Entrées et Soupers

## SNACKS, APPETIZERS AND SUPPER DISHES

Historically, French country households had no use for "appetizers" as we know them: if they ate anything before a meat course it was almost always soup. The evening meal (if it was not yet another substantial *potage*!) might well have been an all-in-one dish of vegetables, perhaps enriched with a cheese sauce, eggs or left-overs. Sometimes such a dish would be promoted to *gratin* status – finished with a savory crumb topping and browned in the oven (leaving *maman* free to continue working until the family came to the table). Pies, pâtés and quiches would be made whenever she had the time, and kept to eat as snacks throughout the day.

LEFT *Beaufort Cheese in production, Savoy*

This chapter contains a number of really versatile old recipes which may be adapted as entrées or one-course meals, as food for picnics or packed lunches, or as courses in a cold buffet.

First, two Burgundian specialties, as simple and useful as the better-known pâtés and terrines. One, looking a bit like head cheese but infinitely more delicious, was traditionally made "from scratch," involving a whole ham and more than a whole day in the kitchen. Our version is quicker and easier. As well as an attractive entrée, it makes a perfect main course with salad.

# Jambon Persillé

### PARSLEYED HAM "CHEESE"
10–12 SLICES

2–2½ lbs *cooked ham, unsliced*
1 cup *jellied chicken stock*★
1 cup *dry white wine*
1–2 *garlic cloves, crushed*
1 tsp each *chopped fresh rosemary and sage ( or pinches of dried)*
1 tbs *chopped fresh tarragon ( or ½ tsp dried)*
*black pepper, freshly ground*
3 tbsp *brandy ( optional)*
2 envelopes *unflavored gelatin*
3 tbsp *chopped parsley*

The famous Bresse chickens are sometimes fattened to produce super-rich livers (*foie blond*), but this next recipe has been adapted to use ordinary chicken livers. Delicately flavored, its texture is somewhere between a pâté and a mousse.

# Gâteau de Foie de Volailles

## CHICKEN LIVER MOLD
SERVES 4–6

½ lb *chicken livers*
1 *small garlic clove*
*salt, pepper, nutmeg*
2 tsp *flour*
¾ cup *heavy cream*
3 *eggs*
15–20 *stuffed or pitted olives*

Rinse and dry the livers and liquidize them with the garlic, adding 2 pinches grated nutmeg, a little salt and pepper and the flour. Sieve. Beat the cream and eggs together and fold into the liver mixture. If the olives are very salty, plunge them into boiling water for a few moments; drain thoroughly.

Butter 4–6 ramekins or a 1 quart soufflé dish (or oil them, lining the bottoms with oiled parchment paper) and pour the mixture in. Place in a roasting pan containing a good 1 inch boiling water and put in a preheated 325°F oven.

After 5 or 10 minutes (for big or small dishes), remove from the oven and quickly add the olives, pressing them gently into the mixture to prevent them floating; return to the oven and continue cooking for 20 (for small) or 30–35 minutes (for large) longer, or until a fine skewer inserted into the middle comes out clean. Unmold carefully.

Traditionally eaten warm with finely sieved tomato sauce*, they are also good cold; in this case you may like to decorate them with sliced olives, blanched button mushrooms or a topping of *foie gras mousse*.

Cut the ham into chunks and put in a pan with the stock, wine, garlic and herbs, if dried. Season with pepper. Bring to a boil and simmer gently for a few minutes to allow the ham to heat through; add the brandy.

Mix the gelatin with 1–2 tbsp water and, when it has dissolved, stir into the ham mixture, off the heat. Cool.

When the mixture starts to thicken, stir in the fresh herbs (including parsley). Spoon the meat into a bowl, terrine or loaf pan, not too tightly packed, pouring the liquid over as you do so, to fill all the spaces. Leave to set. Either unmold or leave in the terrine, if this is attractive. To serve, cut into thick slices with a sharp knife.

Not strictly pâtés, but fulfilling the same role, are *rillettes*. They are made all over France – and from almost any meat, although those from the regions bordering the Loire are the most famous. *Rillettes de Tours* are all pork, *rillettes du Mans* are half goose, *rillettes orléanaises* are half rabbit, and so on.

# Rillettes

### "POTTED PORK"
SERVES 6–10

Trim 1½ lbs lean boneless pork and 1 lb fresh pork sides and cut into cubes. Put in a large flameproof casserole with 3–4 crushed garlic cloves (optional), 2 tsp salt, 1 tsp pepper, a sprig of rosemary or thyme, 1 bay leaf, ½ tsp each grated nutmeg and allspice. Add ¾ cup water and slowly bring to a boil, stirring constantly. Cover tightly and put in a preheated 300°F oven. Cook for 4–5 hours or until all the fat has melted. Stir occasionally, adding a very little more water if needed to prevent sticking; do not boil. Drain, reserving the liquid.

Discard the herbs and shred the meat with two forks until it is even-textured but not smooth. When the liquid is cold, lift off the fat (keep the liquid to flavor soup, etc.) and re-melt it. Stir just enough of the melted fat into the shredded meat to make a thick but spreadable paste. Pack tightly into pots or bowls and cover closely with waxed paper. It will keep in the refrigerator for 1–3 days. Serve with chunks of bread.

If you mean to keep it longer, pack it into canning jars, cover the top of the *rillettes* completely with more melted fat, then seal the jars; they'll keep for 2 weeks or so in the refrigerator.

*Rillettes* of duck or goose (chicken has too bland a flavor) may be made the same way; use the bird's own fat if possible and substitute sage for rosemary or thyme. If you've used the best meat from rabbits or hares for something else, chop the remainder, cover with lard, drippings or bacon fat and proceed in the same way (use thyme to flavor); leave any bones in during cooking, and discard before shredding.

OPPOSITE *Rillons (Crispy Nibbles) and Potted Pork*

If you're making *rillettes*, do consider *rillons* at the same time. I'm afraid the terminology can be rather confusing; *rillons* sometimes mean large chunks of meat cooked similarly to *rillettes* but left whole – when they may also be called *rillauds* or *rillots*! The *rillons* explained here are quite different.

*Grattons* is another word with several meanings. They may be synonymous with *rillons*, or simply fried bacon bits. *Pompes à Grattons* or *Pains aux Grattons* are loaves speckled with these crispy bites.

If you have to skin chicken or other poultry, use the skin for *chicken grattons*. Chop it into small pieces and deep fry them in very hot fat; drain well.

# Rillons

### CRISPY NIBBLES

Cut pork skin, or any fatty trimmings, into bite-size bits. Lay in a roasting pan and cook (on the top shelf of your oven while making *rillettes*, perhaps) until really crisp, spooning off liquid fat from time to time; finish on top of the range if necessary. Drain well and, while still warm, sprinkle with salt, pepper and a little ground allspice. When quite cold, store in screw-top jars before using as cocktail nibbles.

BELOW *Beautiful old river-front houses, Argentat, Limousin*

Many French bakers sell the *gratton* bread described on the previous page; *charcuteries* in some areas specialize in a variety of potato pies. This one, from the southern Alps, makes a good all-in-one supper dish served hot – perhaps with a salad or other vegetable. It was originally a sort of Alpine turnover or portable lunch.

# Tarte de Taillons

## POTATO, BACON AND CHEESE PIE

If to eat cold with the fingers, two beaten eggs poured into the pie before adding the lid will make it more substantial and easier to handle.

pâte brisée* *(see recipe)*
2 lbs *non-floury potatoes*
2 tbsp *oil*
1 *onion, minced*
½ lb *streaky bacon, snipped*
*salt and pepper*
1 *garlic clove, crushed*
¼ lb *cheese thinly sliced*
1 *egg yolk*

Make the pastry dough, using 2¼ cups flour (adjusting other ingredients proportionately) and leave to rest in a cool place.

Wash, peel and cut the potatoes into thin rounds; dry thoroughly. Heat the oil in a large pan and add the potatoes and onion; brown for 5 minutes, turning carefully with a spatula. Remove with a slotted spoon and set aside. Lightly brown the bacon in the same pan, then mix into the potatoes; pepper generously and add a very little salt. Mix in the crushed garlic and the cheese.

Roll out two-thirds of the pastry dough and use to line a deep pie or quiche pan; fill with the mixture. Roll out remaining dough for a lid, seal the edges well and make a criss-cross pattern on top with the point of a knife; glaze with the beaten egg yolk.

Bake in a preheated 400°F oven for 1–1¼ hours, covering the top with foil if it becomes brown too soon.

Good supper dishes come from all over the country. The first two here both contain ham, eggs and cheese but make very different eating – not surprising when you consider the differences between Savoy and the Pays Basque!

The third recipe is a marvelous batter-based concoction from the Auvergne. Isolated housewives added or subtracted according to the state of their pantries and, once you've eaten it, it's easy to see how you can adapt it too. Leftovers are quite acceptable (add a pinch of spice or curry powder); or use bulk sausagemeat (give it a fillip with plenty of chives or some sage); or you can make a green batter as in our recipe.

# Riz à la Bayonnaise

## EGGS BAKED ON HAMMY RICE

1 *large onion, chopped*
2 tbsp *butter*
⅓ cup *diced ham*
1 cup *rice (more if liked)*
1¾ cups *light stock**
*bay leaf*
*salt and pepper*
½ cup *shredded cheese*
4 *eggs*

Soften the onion in the melted butter; add the ham and rice and stir over the heat until the rice turns opaque without coloring. Add the stock, bay leaf and pepper; bring to a boil, stir, cover tightly and simmer for 20 minutes or until the rice is just tender and the liquid absorbed. Taste and add salt if necessary. Take off the heat and leave, covered, for 10 minutes.

Discard the bay leaf and stir in three-quarters of the cheese; check the seasoning. Spoon the mixture into a well-buttered baking dish; make 4 hollows with the back of a spoon, break an egg into each and sprinkle the remaining cheese over. Cover with foil and bake in a preheated 425°F oven for 20 minutes or until egg whites are set and yolks still soft. Serve at once with homemade tomato sauce,* tomatoes oven-baked at the same time or a tossed mixed salad and French bread.

# Pommes Savoyardes

## VEGETABLE, BACON, EGG AND CHEESE BAKE
SERVES 6

6 tbsp *butter or lard*
2 *large onions, sliced*
1 cup *finely chopped Canadian bacon*
1 lb *old potatoes, unpeeled*
¾ lb *carrots*
½ lb *turnips*
*salt and pepper*
6 *eggs*
¾ cup *heavy cream*
1 cup *or more shredded cheese*

Melt the fat in a wide flameproof dish; cook the onions and bacon without browning for 5 minutes. Cut all the vegetables into thick matchsticks and stir them into the dish, adding pepper and a *little* salt. When heated through, cover with foil and cook in a preheated 375°F oven until tender but still crisp – about 20–30 minutes.

Make 6 hollows in the mixture with the back of a spoon. Break an egg into each hollow and cover with heavy cream. Sprinkle shredded cheese over everything, as generously as liked, and return to oven to cook for 8–10 minutes or until the cheese is golden and the eggs are cooked to your liking.

# Pounti

## SAVORY BATTER MEAL
SERVES 10–12 (see **Note** below)

1½ cups *prunes*
1 lb *lean pork, ground or finely chopped*
1 lb *slab bacon, ground or finely chopped*
¾ lb *Swiss chard leaves (or spinach), finely chopped*
3 *onions, chopped*
3–4 tbsp *chopped parsley*
*salt and pepper*
6 *eggs*
1¼ cups *flour*
2¼ cups *milk*
*fat for greasing*

ABOVE *For supper: Pommes Savoyardes (top) and Pounti; savory batter dish with prunes*

Soak the prunes and simmer until plump; pit and halve or quarter them. Mix together the meats, chard leaves (or spinach), onions and parsley to make an *hachis*; season with salt and pepper.

Make a batter by stirring the eggs into the flour, gradually adding most of the milk and beating until smooth.

Pour into the *hachis*, adding the remaining milk if necessary to achieve a thick batter consistency. Check the seasoning.

Turn into a greased roasting pan or high-sided baking dish and press the prunes, evenly spaced, into the mixture. Cook in a preheated 400°F oven for 15 minutes; reduce to 350°F

and cook for a further hour, or until the *pounti* is well browned and risen, and pulling away from the pan at the sides. Serve in large wedges or slices.

**Note**  Don't be nervous of making a lot: it's super (many people prefer it) on the second day – cut into slices and crisp-fried.

Olive oil is not only the main cooking medium of Provence – it's almost a way of life! The photograph shows three old Provençal recipes which feature its uniquely delicious flavor; do use really good quality oil, for full benefit. Traditionally *maigre* dishes (to eat during times of fast, especially before Midnight Mass at Christmas), they make ideal entrées, party food or light snacks.

# Œufs Tapénade

### STUFFED EGGS
SERVES 4–6 AS AN ENTRÉE

*6 hard-cooked eggs*
*6–10 ripe olives, pitted*
*6–8 anchovy fillets, drained*
*2 oz canned tuna fish (about ½ cup)*
*2–3 tbsp capers*
*5–7 tbsp olive oil*
*1–2 tbsp Cognac (optional)*
*lemon juice*
*freshly ground black pepper*
*parsley sprigs or olives for garnish*

Halve the eggs lengthwise, scoop out the yolks and reserve. Using mortar and pestle, food processor or blender, pound the olives, anchovies, tuna and capers to a smooth paste, adding a little oil as you go. Work in more olive oil, a little at a time as for mayonnaise⋆, until the mixture is thick and creamy. Mash the egg yolks and blend them into the mixture. Stir in the Cognac and add a few drops of lemon juice to taste; season with black pepper, no salt.

Pipe the mixture into the egg whites and decorate with tiny sprigs of parsley and a few slices of ripe or green olives.

*Tapéno* is provençal dialect for capers, hence the name. Capers and anchovies alone may be pounded and mixed into olive oil to a mayonnaise⋆ consistency, then sharpened with lemon juice and seasoned with pepper to make a *tapénade* sauce to serve with cold fish or cold meat salad.

LEFT *Olive trees thrive in the stony soil of Provence*
OPPOSITE *Olive Oil and Tomato Omelet, Anchoïade (left) and Stuffed Eggs*

*Anchoïade,* as the name implies, is based on anchovies. When they can't get fresh anchovies, the Provençaux use salted ones: we must make do with canned – which should be thoroughly drained and, if preferred, soaked in milk or water for 30 minutes to counteract excessive salt. There are a great many versions: the photograph shows the simplest.

For 6–8 people, crush and pound 3 small cans anchovy fillets with 3–4 garlic cloves to a smooth paste with a little olive oil (heating may encourage the fish to disintegrate faster). When it's perfectly smooth, stir in more oil until it has the consistency of thick cream. Season with black pepper.

Use as a dip for raw vegetables (celery, cauliflower florets, Belgian endive, etc.), accompanied by chunks of French bread. Or toast one side of bread slices, spread the *anchoïade* on the other and heat in a preheated 400°F oven for 10 minutes or so. Or spread it on rolled-out pastry, bread or pizza dough, and bake in a very hot oven until the base is cooked through.

Finally, while on the subject of olive oil, a tomato omelet which is redolent of the Midi. Be sure to preheat the oven to hottest before you begin and warm up an ovenproof plate for each diner; use an omelet pan of the same size.

# Omelette à l'Huile d'Olive et aux Tomates

### OMELET WITH OLIVE OIL AND TOMATOES
SERVES 1

Beat 2 eggs with 1 tbsp olive oil, salt, pepper and 1–2 tbsp *tomate concassée*★. Heat 2 tbsp olive oil in the pan and, when very hot, pour in the egg mixture; stir it around with a fork until it starts to set – about ½ minute.

Slide the omelet onto a warmed plate, sprinkle with 2–3 sliced pitted olives and put into the very hot oven to finish cooking and puff up, 1–2 minutes. Sprinkle with parsley and run with it to the table. Eat immediately.

ABOVE *Cheese, Bread and Potato Omelet*

Cheese omelets are invaluable as a quick, nourishing and cheap vegetarian meal. In France's eastern mountains they still make dozens of delicious cheeses, and cheese omelets are understandably popular. In the village of Les Andrieux, so deep in a Dauphinois valley that the sun doesn't light the streets for three months of the year, cheese omelets used to feature in an annual rite that dates from ancient times.

Before dawn on 10 February, shepherds blew a fife and trumpet fanfare to announce the return of the light after a hundred days' absence. The villagers made cheese omelets, took them in procession to lay on the parapet of the bridge and ritually danced for joy (and, doubtless, to keep warm) in a nearby field. When the sun's rays finally lit the scene, they returned to the bridge and dedicated the omelets to the heavenly body before taking them home and eating them. They must have been pretty tough by then!

Here's a better recipe, which only needs a salad to make a smashing meal-in-one. (Make garlic butter by softening finely chopped garlic in butter *very slowly* – it burns easily – until it starts to brown; strain out the bits.)

# Omelette à la Savoyarde

## CHEESE, BREAD AND POTATO OMELET
### SERVES 2–3 AS A SUPPER DISH, MORE AS AN APPETIZER

$\frac{1}{4}$ cup *oil*
$\frac{1}{4}$ cup *garlic butter (see above)*
2 *cooked potatoes, diced*
2 *large slices of bread, diced*
3–4 tbsp *butter or other fat*
6 *eggs*
*salt and pepper*
*chopped chervil or parsley*
$\frac{1}{2}$ cup *finely diced cheese*

Heat the oil and garlic butter together, and when hot add the potato dice. After a few moments add the bread; fry briskly until golden brown. Distribute evenly in the pan and add the remaining fat.

Beat the eggs lightly, and season with salt, pepper and chosen herbs. Make the omelet as usual and add the cheese as soon as it starts to set. Turn off the heat, fold the omelet in two and leave in the pan for 1–2 minutes for the cheese to melt.

Eggs are among the world's most popular quick-meal ingredients, and omelets are one of the most interesting ways of cooking them. Once you can make one, you can make dozens without further recipes – simply by filling them with any leftovers your refrigerator may be harboring.

Here's another hearty mountain dish: *matafans*, an Alpine tradition going back to the Middle Ages. The name comes from an old dialect word, *mata-fame*, meaning "kill-hunger" – or breakfast.

# Matafan Savoyard de Printemps

## SPRING SPINACH OMELET
SERVES 3–4

1 lb *spinach*
*salt and pepper*
¼ cup *butter*
3–4 *eggs*
1 heaping tbsp *flour*
4–5 tbsp *milk*

Trim the spinach, wash well and squeeze out all water. Put in a pan with a sprinkle of salt and cook covered for 10 minutes (lift the lid and turn the spinach several times). Drain, pressing out all moisture; chop.

Heat the butter in a large frying pan and lay the spinach over the bottom; beat the eggs into the flour, stir in the milk and pour into the pan. Season well, and prod with a fork to allow the egg mixture to run through the spinach.

When it starts to solidify, turn the *matafan* carefully and brown the other side. Serve at once.

The winter version was altogether more hearty, and could be made even more so by adding diced cooked ham and cheese or other meat, fried bacon snips, or even dried fruit. In my opinion these also make it more appetizing; here is the *basic* recipe:

# Matafans d'Hiver

## POTATO PANCAKES
SERVES 2–4

Mix 1¾ cups grated raw floury potato with 1 cup flour; beat in 2 eggs and enough milk to make a pancake-like batter. Season well.

Heat butter and oil in a frying pan and when hot pour in spoonfuls of the mixture to make pancakes of ½ inch thick; cook for 4–5 minutes before turning to brown the other side. If adding "extras" (see above), spread them on the pancakes as soon as the batter is in the pan.

BELOW *Spinach Omelet (left) and Potato Pancakes*

Never imagine that *œufs en cocotte* are "just baked eggs." Smoothed with cream and imaginatively flavoured, they can be ambrosial. Our first recipe is actually designed to be cooked *on top of* the range, though you can use the oven if you like. If you've no small ramekins, the second recipe is for eggs baked with cream and cheese in an *edible* pot.

# Œufs aux Herbes

### HERBY BAKED EGGS

3 tbsp *butter*
4 *eggs*
1 cup *heavy cream or* crème fraîche★
½ tsp *cornstarch*
1–2 tbsp *chopped parsley*
1–2 tbsp *chopped chives*
*salt and pepper*

Divide the butter among 4 individual ramekins or heatproof dishes and melt it slowly in a large double boiler or water bath over a very low heat. Break an egg into each, cover and cook as gently as possible.

Meanwhile, put the cream over a medium heat to reduce. Mix the cornstarch with 2 tsp water and stir into the cream; continue cooking until slightly thickened. Stir in the herbs and season to taste.

When the eggs are just set, spoon the sauce over and serve at once.

# Tomates Cocotte

### TOMATO POTS

4 *large firm tomatoes*
*salt and pepper*
¾ cup *shredded cheese*
4 *eggs*
¼ cup *heavy cream*
3 tbsp *butter*

Cut the tops off the tomatoes with a sharp knife; remove cores and seeds. Sprinkle the insides with salt; turn upside-down on paper towels to drain for 30 minutes.

Blot as much moisture as you can from the interior of each tomato and make 4 small slits around the top with a sharp knife. Cook for 5 minutes in a preheated 450°F oven. Remove and put 2 tbsp cheese into each. Break an egg into each tomato and season. Heat the cream to boiling point and spoon it

ABOVE *Herby Baked Eggs (top) and cheesy Tomato Pots*

onto the eggs; top with a pat of butter and the remaining cheese. Bake for a further 5–10 minutes.

*Aiglefin* is French for haddock, but for some reason the fish when smoked is known as *haddock*. You can also use smoked cod for this recipe from the inventive Basques.

# Haddock à la Basquaise

## SMOKED HADDOCK SUPPER
SERVES 4–6

Take 1 lb smoked haddock (finnan haddie) and poach in milk till tender, 8–10 minutes (if very dry soak in milk first). Drain, skin, trim and flake the fish. Gently cook 1 lb thinly sliced potatoes in 3 tbsp oil till tender. Add 2 cups homemade tomato sauce★ and mix in 1–2 chopped garlic cloves and a handful of chopped parsley. Fold in fish and heat all together for 10 minutes. Serve in a big shallow bowl garnished with ripe olives.

Roscoff, famous as a ferry port, has less commercial charms too. And it's in the heart of Brittany's "vegetable garden:" hundreds of tons of artichokes and cauliflowers are auctioned at the nearby Kerisnel co-operative each day. An exciting business, rather like a *grand prix* for tractors, it's worth an early start to watch.

# Salade Roscovite

## ROSCOFF SALAD
SERVES 6–8 AS AN ENTRÉE

1 *cucumber*
*salt*
1 *large cauliflower*
¾ lb (about 2 pints) *cooked shrimp (unshelled)*
1 cup *mayonnaise*★
6 tbsp *vinaigrette*★
2 *cooked potatoes, peeled and sliced*
2 *hard-cooked eggs (optional)*

Wash and finely slice the unpeeled cucumber. Put in a colander with plenty of salt; leave to drain for 20–30

ABOVE *Roscoff Salad combines shrimp with cooked and raw vegetables*

minutes, then rinse and wipe quite dry. Cut the cauliflower into florets and cook in boiling salted water until tender but still *al dente* – 5–8 minutes. Reserve a few unshelled shrimp, and shell and devein the rest. Mix a third of the mayonnaise with the vinaigrette.

Combine the cucumber, cauliflower, shelled shrimp and potato slices in a large bowl; toss gently in the dressing. Serve decorated with unshelled shrimp and slices of hard-cooked egg (if using). Hand the remaining mayonnaise separately.

127

One of the peasant wife's most useful standbys was stuffed cabbage, which appears as part of the local diet from Brittany to Provence. It was a way of using up leftover meat, and if there was no meat of any kind it could be stuffed with a bread-and-cheese mixture, or with other vegetables, crumbs and herbs. Single large leaves could be wrapped for individual portions, or the whole cabbage stuffed, to make a more impressive-looking dish.

*Chou farci*, stuffed cabbage, has many local names, such as the old Provençal dialect *sou fassum* or the most delightful of all – *la poule verte*, meaning "green hen."

The stuffing can be made, in fact, with whatever you fancy or have handy. For a whole cabbage, the stuffing should weigh *approximately* one-third of the cabbage's weight. But don't be afraid of making too much; any excess may be rolled into meatballs and boiled or fried, served with tomato sauce★ (or in another soup), or wrapped in pastry and baked for picnics or lunchboxes. Uncooked stuffing could also be mixed with onions, peppers and tomatoes and baked in a pastry case to make a savory starter or to serve with salad as a light meal.

# Chou Farci

## STUFFED CABBAGE

SERVES 4–6

1 *large head cabbage*
1½ cups *ground or chopped lean pork*
½ cup *ground or chopped bacon or ham*
½ cup *bulk pork sausagemeat*
2 *chicken livers, ground or finely chopped*
1 *large slice day-old bread, soaked in milk*
2 tbsp *tomato paste*
2 *garlic cloves, crushed*
2 *shallots, chopped, or 2 tbsp chopped chives or scallion*
2 *onions, chopped*
2 tbsp *chopped parsley*
1 tbsp *dried herbs (according to taste)*
*juice and grated rind of ½ lemon*
2 tsp *salt, and pepper*
1 *egg*

Trim any broken leaves from the cabbage, and cut out some of the stalk with an apple-corer. Put in a pan of boiling salted water and cook gently for 5–10 minutes; drain well.

Thoroughly squeeze out the bread and mix with all the remaining ingredients.

Without pulling them off, carefully separate and open out the cabbage leaves as far as you can. Cut out the heart and fill the space with stuffing. Then spoon the *farce* into the spaces between the leaves, folding the leaf-tops back towards the center as you go; you'll finish with a rather large squat-looking cabbage. Secure it, not too tightly; you could ease it into a cotton net in which fruit or vegetables have been sold – or bind it neatly several times, with cotton tape.

Traditionally served in vegetable soup (e.g. *Soupe d'automme* (p. 15)) or in a *pot-au-feu* (p. 66) in place of *mique*, the cabbage may also simply be simmered, lightly covered, for about an hour in well-flavored stock. Alternatively, fit the cabbage snugly into an earthenware casserole (pour ¾ inch stock into the casserole first) or wrap in greased foil and bake for 1 hour in a preheated 350°F oven. If the cabbage appears to dry out during cooking, spoon a little stock into the casserole or open up the foil and pour some stock in. Either way, remove wrappings to serve. If not part of soup etc., serve with homemade tomato sauce★.

BELOW *Stuffed Cabbage in its different forms*

To make a convincing *poule verte*, cook cabbage 5–8 minutes and remove 8–12 outer leaves. Lay these, overlapping, on a counter top. Shape the stuffing into a fat football shape, lay it on the center of the cabbage leaves and wrap it up, first turning the ends in, then folding up the long sides. Bind securely. Cook for at least an hour as above.

For individual *choux*, blanch the cabbage as before and peel off as many outer leaves as you require *choux*. Wrap appropriate amounts of stuffing in the single leaves (or use two leaves together if they are rather small) and tie securely. Place in a single layer in a large pan and pour in boiling stock to $\frac{1}{2}$ inch; cover and simmer for 20–30 minutes. These also may be served in a vegetable soup or are often added to a *garbure navarraise* (p. 18) instead of the *confit*.

The French word *rissoles* means fried pastry turnovers, and they are another excellent way of using any stuffing leftover from the *chou farci*. If there scarcely seems enough, bulk it out with chopped leftover (cooked) veal or poultry, add more minced onion or parsley and cook all together over a low heat for 5–8 minutes. Bind with another egg if necessary.

Roll out *pâte brisée*★ and cut out 4 inch rounds; put a spoonful of *farce* on each; fold over and seal tightly. Deep-fry in very hot oil until the pastry is crisp; drain and serve hot.

# Rissoles de St Flour

### CHEESE TURNOVERS
MAKES 15–20

Roll out *pâte brisée*★ (quantity as for p. 138) and cut into 4 inch rounds.

Mix together $\frac{1}{2}$ cup cottage curd or cream cheese, $\frac{1}{2}$ cup shredded Gruyère, Swiss or Cheddar cheese, 1 large or 2 small eggs, 2 tsp chopped chives and 1 tsp chopped parsley; season with salt and pepper. Divide the filling between the pastry rounds, fold them over and seal the edges with water; chill until firm.

Deep-fry for about 5–6 minutes in hot oil; serve hot or warm.

A Burgundian version of the same snack is known as *corniottes* – they look rather like little cocked hats.

In this case use flaky pastry and cut it into 5 inch rounds. Put spoonfuls of the same filling (with or without herbs) onto the centers, then fold up from three sides to make a tricorne shape; pinch tightly to seal securely. Place on a dampened baking sheet, glaze with beaten egg and chill until firm before baking in a preheated 400°F oven for 15 minutes. Remove and sprinkle carefully with more shredded cheese; return to the oven and bake for 5–10 minutes longer until golden brown. Eat hot or warm.

In the eastern mountains of Savoy and Dauphiné, they have their own local cheeses which they use to make similar snacks. In the Jura they stuff rolls (day-old ones are fine) to make their version.

For *Petits Pains à la Jurassienne*, halve rolls laterally or cut off the tops, according to size and shape, and scoop out most of the crumb (or cut 2 inch thick slices of bread and hollow them to make a "box"). Optionally, sprinkle the insides with a little dry white wine.

Make a thick béchamel sauce★ and stir in plenty of grated cheese (if liked, add diced cooked ham and sliced mushrooms too); fill rolls with this. Scatter more grated cheese on them and bake in a hot oven until well heated and bubbly on top.

Cheese of course is endlessly useful for quick snacks and light meals; the same dishes can also be used as entrées or as savories. (I quite often serve some of these *before* dessert, French fashion, if I think there'll be red wine still unfinished after the meat course.)

*Camembert en Surprise* lives up to its name and could hardly be simpler. Allow 1 whole Camembert (choose them only just ripe) for 3–4 people as an appetizer, or for 2 as a supper dish to eat with plain vegetables or a lemon-dressed tossed salad.

Simply roll out two rounds of flaky pastry – one thin and one very thin – for each cheese (1–1½ inches larger than it). Place the cheese on one, moisten the edges and cover with the second; seal, pressing down hard all around with fork tines. Make a few evaporation holes on top, brush with melted butter and bake in a preheated 425°F oven for 20 minutes until the pastry is browned and well risen.

Camembert is France's own most popular cheese, excellent for dessert or snacks. If you're fond of it too, try these Norman fritters. They could be an entrée or part of a buffet supper.

# Croquettes au Camembert

MAKES 15–20

Make a roux with 6 tbsp butter and $\frac{1}{2}$ cup flour; stir in $1\frac{1}{2}$ cups milk to make a thick sauce. Cut the rind off $\frac{1}{2}$ lb Camembert; chop the cheese and stir into the sauce over a low heat until smooth. Add 2 tsp Dijon-style mustard, and salt, pepper and nutmeg to taste. Pour into buttered jelly roll pans (about $\frac{1}{2}$ inch thick) and chill overnight.

Cut into squares; dust with flour. Dip into a mixture of 1 egg beaten with 1 tbsp each water and oil, then coat with dry crumbs. Deep fry quickly in very hot oil and drain on paper towels; serve with fried parsley.

LEFT *Petits Pains à la Jurassienne (left) and Corniottes*

*Quiche Lorraine* is world-famous, but other quiches are just as good. Try Aveyron's super two-cheese quiche:

# Quiche aux Deux Fromages

### TWO-CHEESE QUICHE
SERVES 4–6 AS A SUPPER DISH, 6–8 AS AN APPETIZER

Line a 10 inch flan ring or quiche pan with *pâte brisée*★ and leave in a cool place.

Beat 2 large eggs into 1½ cups heavy cream or *crème fraîche*★. Season with salt, pepper and nutmeg; strain. Cover the bottom of the pastry case with 1½ cups shredded Cheddar cheese; crumble over ½ lb Roquefort or other blue cheese. Pour in the cream mixture and bake in a preheated 475°F oven for 20–25 minutes.

Next, a simple but decorative piquant tomato quiche. The amount of mustard depends on your taste and the type used.

# Tarte à la Tomate

### PIQUANT TOMATO QUICHE
SERVES 4–6

*pâte feuilletée*★
*mustard (see above)*
½ lb *hard cheese*
6–8 *tomatoes*
*salt and black pepper*

Line a 10 inch flan ring or quiche pan with the thinly-rolled pastry dough; spread the bottom with mustard. Cut the cheese into fine slices and cover the mustard.

Remove any hard cores from the tomatoes, cut them into slices or wedges and arrange neatly in the pastry case. Season with pepper and a little salt; sprinkle with thyme. Bake in a preheated 450°F oven for 30–35 minutes.

LEFT *Piquant Tomato Quiche*

ABOVE *Pears stuffed with a sophisticated mixture of brandy, crème fraîche and Roquefort cheese*

# Tarte aux Noix de Périgord

## SAVORY WALNUT QUICHE

Line a 7 inch quiche pan with *pâte brisée*★; soak ½ cup soft fresh bread crumbs briefly in a little water and then squeeze out. Mix them with ¾ cup chopped walnuts and ¼ cup chopped parsley; add 2 eggs beaten with 6 tbsp each milk and heavy cream. Season with salt, pepper and nutmeg and pour into the pastry case; sprinkle with 1 tbsp grated cheese and bake in a preheated 360°F oven for 40–45 minutes or until set and lightly browned. Best eaten hot.

Finally, our own walnut favorite: a sophisticated yet exquisitely simple idea good enough to start – or finish – an important dinner party:

# Poires au Roquefort

## STUFFED PEARS

SERVES 4 AS AN ENTRÉE,
8 AS A SNACK

1 cup *shelled walnuts*
¼ lb *Roquefort cheese*
2 tbsp *Cognac*
*heavy cream or* crème fraîche *(see recipe)*
4 *ripe pears*
*shelled and peeled pistachio nuts (optional)*

Reserve 8 perfect walnut halves; mill or grind the rest. Mix them with the mashed cheese, Cognac and enough cream (about ¼ cup) to make a thick paste; chill for 30 minutes.

Peel, halve and core pears, making large cavities (if not to be eaten immediately, brush them all over with lemon-and-water to prevent browning). Fill the centers with the mixture (prettiest if you use a pastry bag); decorate with the reserved walnuts and pistachio nuts. (Any leftover filling may be thinned with more cream, *crème fraîche*, sour cream or yogurt to make a party dip.)

131

# Reference File

Containing the many basic methods and recipes (sauces, stocks, pastries, doughs and so on) which recur throughout the book.

## Crème Fraîche

The literal meaning of this is "fresh cream" and, indeed, if you have unpasteurized cream, that's exactly what it is – with no need to do anything to it at all. Pasteurization removes quite a lot of the lactic acid and natural ferments which give "fresh" cream its distinctive taste and which make it thicken a little more each day (and, of course, which eventually turn it sour).

Because really old recipes naturally used *crème fraîche* as it was the cream from home farm milk, traditionalists still use it. If you can buy only pasteurized cream, this treatment will give it an authentic, natural taste. Here is a distillation of a number of recognized methods:

2 cups *heavy cream*
1 cup *buttermilk, sour cream or plain yogurt (buttermilk is said to produce the best flavor, yogurt keeps longest)*

Mix together and heat slowly to 75°F. Transfer to a container in which you can keep it as near to this temperature for as long as possible – a thermos or a warmed jar which you can wrap all around and cover with a towel. Keep overnight in a warm place. Stir, cover firmly and chill. It should keep for at least 2 weeks or longer in the refrigerator.

*Crème fraîche* has a pleasant, slightly fermented and nutty taste; it cooks well and can be boiled at length without curdling. Good quality heavy cream has all these qualities except the taste, and may safely be substituted for *crème fraîche* – as may freshly-soured cream where liked.

# Crème Pâtissière

## CONFECTIONER'S CUSTARD OR PASTRY CREAM

This is invaluable for keeping juices from soaking into the pastry of a tart case and making it soggy (though it should itself not be spread on the pastry too long before serving). It also has many other uses.

The good old-fashioned way of adding vanilla flavor is to put a vanilla bean in the milk, heat it just to boiling, then leave it to infuse until cool. Alternatively, *either* use vanilla sugar instead of plain, *or* add a few drops of vanilla towards the end of the procedure.

*2 egg yolks*
*¼ cup sugar (see above)*
*6 tbsp cornstarch, flour or a mixture of both*
*1½ cups milk (see above)*
*1 egg white*
*vanilla bean or extract (see above)*

Beat yolks and sugar together until frothy. Sift the cornstarch and/or flour into another bowl; blend in the egg mixture with 2–3 tbsp milk. Bring the remaining milk just to a boil and pour onto the mixture, stirring continuously; return to milk pan and stir over gentle heat until thickened and almost boiling. Set aside.

Beat the egg white until stiff; put one-quarter of the custard into a bowl, fold the white in carefully and then fold all back into the remaining custard. Cook gently on very gentle heat, folding the custard over lightly; this helps it to cook to a very light consistency.

# Tomate Concassée

Literally "crushed tomato," *tomate concassée* is a useful kitchen basic of which professional kitchens keep a permanent stock on hand.

OPPOSITE *Gleaming utensils in the kitchen fireplace in the hospice at Baune*

Fry 4 grated shallots (or 1 grated onion) in ¼ cup butter (or 2 tbsp oil) for 2–3 minutes. Add 1½–2 cups skinned, seeded and roughly chopped tomatoes, 4 crushed garlic cloves, 2 sprigs thyme (or ½ tsp dried), 3 bay leaves and 1 tsp sugar. Cook, uncovered, over medium heat for 15 minutes, stirring occasionally. Keep in a bowl or jar for use as required, to improve the flavor of soups, stews, egg dishes and so on.

More simply, just mix all the above ingredients together without cooking. Naturally, this mixture can be made up immediately before use but, especially if there is little or no further cooking involved, the flavors will mingle better if made at least an hour or two in advance.

# Petit Salé

## HOME-CURED PORK
SERVES 6–8

The name means "lightly-salted." Pork treated thus will keep up to 2 weeks in the refrigerator or overnight in a cool place.

*1 heaping tsp chopped fresh thyme (or pinch dried)*
*bay leaf*
*1–2 garlic cloves, sliced*
*12 juniper berries*
*1 clove*
*1⅓ cups gros sel (sea salt)*
*¼ cup saltpeter*
*50 g/2 oz sugar*
*2½ lbs fresh pork arm picnic roast, or 4½ lbs country-style ribs*

Start this at least one day before you intend to eat it.

Bring 2 cups water to a boil, add the herbs, garlic and spices and simmer for 10 minutes. Meanwhile, dissolve the salt, saltpeter and sugar in 1½ quarts water, stirring over gentle heat. Strain the herb water into this and leave to cool.

Put the meat into a large non-metal bowl or container, cover with the curing liquid and leave, covered, until needed. If used after 3 days or less, rinse well under cold water before cooking. If it has been in the brine longer, soak in cold water for 1 hour for each week's curing.

# Basic Marinade

A marinade is a flavored liquid in which meats or fish may be soaked before cooking (fish marinades are mainly lemon juice). The main purpose of this marinade, for game or meat, is to tenderize and/or to help it "keep." At the same time, the meat is impregnated with a new flavor.

If your game or meat is fresh, young, tender and tasty, by all means regard a marinade as *optional*. If you omit it, and your recipe later calls for marinade ingredients in a sauce or gravy, simply follow the instructions using equivalent amounts of *fresh* vegetables and wine etc. instead.

Adjust quantities according to the size of the cut to be marinated: this should be enough for a leg of (roe) venison – or lamb; obviously you'll need less for a rabbit, less still for a saddle of hare.

*2 carrots, sliced*
*2 onions, sliced*
*2 stalks celery, sliced (optional)*
*3 shallots, sliced (optional)*
*bay leaf, thyme and parsley or 1–2 bouquets garni*
*12 black peppercorns, lightly crushed*
*1 tbsp juniper berries, lightly crushed*
*1 tsp salt*
*2 tbsp brandy (optional)*
*nutmeg*
*4–5 strips orange or lemon peel (optional)*
*2 garlic cloves, crushed*
*2 cloves (optional)*
*¼ cup oil*
*1 quart red wine – or enough to cover meat*

**Note** Several items are listed as optional – but clearly the more flavors in the marinade, the more tasty the meat.

Unless otherwise instructed in the recipe, mix all the ingredients together in a non-metal bowl and soak the meat overnight, turning it every few hours.

If your recipe calls for a *cooked marinade*: lightly brown the vegetables in the oil for a few minutes, stir in the remaining ingredients and moisten with the wine. Simmer for at least 30 minutes, then *let it cool* completely before soaking the meat.

# SAUCES

# Sauce Tomate

## TOMATO SAUCE

This sauce may be sieved, milled, liquidized – or left "rough" (I prefer the latter). If you are going to sieve it, there's no need to skin, seed and core the tomatoes.

¼ cup *olive oil*
2–3 *large onions, chopped*
2–5 *garlic cloves, crushed*
2¼ lbs *ripe tomatoes, skinned, seeded and roughly chopped*
1–2 *sprigs fresh basil, tarragon or thyme or bouquet garni*
2 tbsp *chopped parsley*
*salt and pepper*

Heat the oil in a large pan and cook the onions gently until soft. When the onions begin to soften, stir in the garlic and, after a few minutes, the tomatoes, herbs and seasoning. Cook over medium heat, stirring occasionally, for about 25 minutes, adding the parsley towards the end of cooking time. The sauce should be fairly thick, with tomatoes reduced to an even purée. Mill or liquidize if liked (remove herb stalks or bouquet first).

This sauce freezes well, or may be kept in sterilized canning jars.

BELOW *Onion seller carved on a church in Roscoff*

# Mayonnaise

A basic recipe, to which some people like to add a little cream. Many other sauces are based on mayonnaise including *Aïoli* and *Sauce Gribiche*.

2 *egg yolks*
½ tsp *Dijon-style mustard*
½ tsp *salt*
½ tsp *sugar*
*pinch white pepper*
*pinch cayenne*
1 tsp *lemon juice*
1 cup *olive oil*
2 tbsp *white wine vinegar*

Have ingredients at room temperature, not straight from the refrigerator. Place the yolks in a bowl and beat or whisk for a few moments to smooth and slightly thicken them. Add seasonings and lemon juice.

Now add about 2 tbsp oil, a few drops at a time, stirring quickly with a small wooden spoon (use a blender if liked). As the mixture becomes very thick, dilute it with a tsp or so of the vinegar, then continue to add oil, in a thin stream or a few drops at a time, stirring continuously and thinning with vinegar as required. The amount of vinegar needed depends partly on your taste and partly on the thickness of mayonnaise required: true mayonnaise "stands up by itself" and is quite bland. If using a blender, you may use *whole* eggs, especially if you prefer a slightly lighter mayonnaise.

# Aïoli

## GARLICKY MAYONNAISE

So popular in the southeast that it is sometimes known as *beurre de Provence* (Provençal butter), *aïoli* may be used as an alternative to mayonnaise for garlic-lovers but has many other – better – uses. It may be served with hot or cold fish or shellfish, with hot or cold boiled beef, with potatoes or other vegetables (separately or together, hot or cold), with snails – in fact, with almost anything that has been plainly cooked.

As there is no point in making *aïoli* if you don't like garlic, make it the Provençal way:

Crush and pound 5–10 garlic cloves (according to size) in a mortar or heavy bowl, then add egg yolks and proceed exactly as for mayonnaise, using all lemon juice rather than lemon and vinegar.

Another cold sauce, famous throughout France, which helps to give a new meaning to cold meat or cold fish:

# Sauce Gribiche

SERVES ABOUT 6

Separate 3 hard-cooked eggs. Mash the yolks in a bowl with 1 tbsp mustard (see p. 22), 1 tbsp vinegar, salt and pepper. Add 1 cup oil a little at a time, as for mayonnaise★.

Chop a small bunch of parsley, 3 sprigs of tarragon and 6–10 chive spikes (only fresh herbs will do); roughly chop the egg whites. Fold all into the sauce and serve cold.

If you like a highly seasoned sauce, add a *little* chili powder or cayenne.

# Sauce Vinaigrette

## FRENCH DRESSING

This is a fairly representative basic recipe. Naturally you can make variations to suit yourself: add more garlic; add 1–2 tsp chopped fresh herbs; add some minutely chopped scallion; substitute all lemon juice for vinegar (in which case you may need more sugar) – and so on.

½ tsp *salt*
¼–½ tsp *pepper*
1 tsp *Dijon-style mustard*
1 tsp *sugar*
1 *garlic clove, crushed*
¾ cup *olive oil*
¼ cup *wine vinegar or vinegar and lemon juice*

Mix the salt, pepper, mustard, sugar and garlic to a paste. Whisk in the olive oil, then stir in the vinegar and/or lemon juice. If to be used for dressing lettuce, leave until just before serving and whisk again before adding to salad.

# Sauce Béchamel

True béchamel sauce is a delicious creation, requiring rather a lot of time and trouble. At the other end of the scale is the more familiar cream or white sauce which is a pallid roux thinned with milk and "flavored" only with salt and pepper.

For most purposes, and particularly if it is not to stand in its own right, this compromise is quite adequate:

1 *blade of mace (or small pinch of powdered)*
1 *bay leaf*
1 *small shallot, quartered*
4–5 *black peppercorns*
1¼ cups *milk*
2 tbsp *butter*
2 tbsp *flour*
2 tbsp *cream (see recipe)*
*salt and pepper*

BELOW *Raw vegetables can be enlivened with Aïoli, Sauce Gribiche, or Sauce Fraîche*

Put the first four ingredients in a pan, cover with milk and bring slowly to a boil. Turn off heat at once; leave to infuse for *at least* 15 minutes.

Melt the butter in a small pan; stir in the flour, off the heat; cook gently for a moment or two but don't let it color. Pour on the strained milk and stir very thoroughly until quite smooth. Simmer very gently for 2–3 minutes, adding the cream (or make up the quantity with more milk). Taste and season.

# Sauce Romesco

A highly-seasoned sauce of Spanish origin, this is particularly popular along the western Mediterranean coast as an accompaniment to hot or cold fish, shellfish etc. It is often served in tandem with *aïoli*.

1 lb *ripe tomatoes*
2 *bulbs garlic (perhaps rather less for American tastes!)*
2 *sweet red peppers, halved*
¾ cup *olive oil*
1 *large slice crustless bread fried in oil, or*
  ½ cup *chopped toasted almonds*
½ cup *vinegar*
½ tsp *freshly ground black pepper*
*salt and cayenne*

Brush the tomatoes, garlic and peppers all over with some of the oil. Place on a flat tray and turn them under the broiler until they are hot through and the outsides are beginning to char; brush them from time to time with more oil if they seem to be drying out.

Put them, still hot, into a mortar and crush them thoroughly, together with the fried bread or almonds (this can be done in a blender or food processor, but remove the tomato and garlic skins first). When fairly smooth, incorporate the vinegar and black pepper. Add the remaining oil, a little at a time, working the sauce continually. Add salt and cayenne to taste (it should be highly seasoned, but not so "hot" as to burn the mouth).

Pass through a sieve, pressing well, or continue to liquidize.

Refrigerate for at least 2 hours. Stir well and check seasoning just before serving.

A very delicious English sauce which is less often eaten today than it once was – perhaps because it traditionally accompanied mutton, which is rarely seen nowadays – is onion sauce. As with mint sauce, I have found a French version which is very different, and just right for broiled beef and pork dishes.

# Sauce aux Oignons

## ONION SAUCE

Slice 6 medium/large onions very finely and soften them gently in ¼ cup butter, stirring often. When they're cooked and golden but not brown, stir in 2 heaping tbsp mustard (see p. 22); mix well, then add ½ cup *crème fraîche*★. (If you substitute heavy cream, use a slightly sharper mustard.) Season to taste with salt and pepper and heat thoroughly. If it should become too thick before serving, stir in a very little hot water.

# Sauce aux Châtaignes

## CHESTNUT SAUCE

A traditional accompaniment for game, particularly venison, this is also excellent with turkey, chicken and other poultry.

1 lb *peeled chestnuts*★
2 cups *game, meat or poultry stock*★
1 *medium-size onion, sliced*
*salt, pepper, bouquet garni*
3–4 tbsp *heavy cream or* crème fraîche★

Cook the peeled chestnuts in the stock with the onion and bouquet garni for 30–45 minutes or until really tender; discard bouquet garni, and mill or liquidize to a purée. Taste and season. Return to the heat, stir in cream and cook gently until desired consistency is reached.

(If preferred – for instance, if the meal is very rich – omit the cream and thicken the sauce by making a white roux and adding the puréed chestnuts.)

The French tend to consider our mint jelly somewhat barbaric – certainly too sweet for the delicate taste of lamb. (I admit that I can see their point, especially if the lamb is cold.) However, they do use mint in sauces for meat dishes; here are two:

# Sauce Fraîche

## "FRESH SAUCE" (for broiled meats or kabobs)

2 cups *plain yogurt*
3–4 heaping tbsp *chopped fresh mint*
1 *very small chili pepper, crushed to paste (or to powder if dry) or* 1 tsp *cayenne*
*salt*

Beat ingredients together; add salt to taste. Pour into a serving bowl and chill for 2 hours before serving decorated with a sprinkling of paprika and a few mint leaves.

ABOVE *Castelbouc nestling in the bottom of the Tarn Gorge*

# Sauce Pauloise

## "SAUCE FROM PAU" (in the Pyrenees)

2 tbsp *chopped mint*
5 *shallots (or 2 onions), finely chopped*
½ cup *white wine vinegar*
3 *egg yolks*
*salt and pepper*
1 cup (½ lb) *butter (chilled)*

Put the mint, shallots or onions and vinegar into a small pan over high heat; stir until liquid has evaporated, being careful not to let it burn. Remove from heat and whisk in the yolks, 2 tbsp water, salt and pepper. Place saucepan over another full of boiling water (or transfer to double boiler) and heat gently while whisking in the butter, cut in small pieces, a little at a time.

# STOCKS

Good quality stock makes all the difference to cooking, especially if the dish is a simple one. Stock made from cubes, or canned broth, will add good flavor – generally adequate for soups or for dishes which have other thickening – but they will not provide the "body" texture needed for some dishes.

Homemade stocks freeze well; make a large quantity and divide into smaller ones for convenience. They will also keep for several days in the refrigerator, but should be re-boiled in a clean pan for a few minutes every day.

*Fond* is the French word for stock. A *fond blanc*★ (white stock) is generally made with veal bones; *fond brun*★ is brown stock and has a stronger flavor.

# Fond Blanc

## VEAL STOCK
### YIELD APPROX. 2 QUARTS

Place $2\frac{1}{4}$ lbs veal shank (or ask your butcher for other suitable bones) in a pan; cover with cold water. Bring to a boil and cook for 5–10 minutes, then drain.

Put the bones back in the rinsed pan, together with 2 sliced onions, 2 sliced carrots, 2 chopped celery stalks, a bouquet garni, salt, a few white peppercorns and a squeeze of lemon juice. Add $2\frac{1}{2}$ quarts cold water, bring to a boil, cover and simmer for 2–3 hours. Strain, cool and skim off fat.

# Fond de Volaille

## CHICKEN STOCK
### YIELD APPROX. 2 QUARTS

The best chicken stock of all is made by putting a whole dressed and drawn stewing chicken into a large pot with the giblets and neck, 1–2 sliced onions, 2–3 sliced carrots, a chopped leek (and a chopped turnip if available), bouquet garni, a few black peppercorns and some salt. Cover generously with about

$2\frac{1}{2}$ quarts cold water, bring to a boil, cover and simmer for 2–3 hours or until the bird starts to fall apart.

(The snag with this method is that the chicken meat gives up most of its flavor to the stock and is afterwards really only suitable for feeding the cat – but it *is* superb.)

Excellent stock is also made as the by-product of cooking a stewing chicken for eating. Proceed as above but simmer only until the bird is tender right through – 1–$1\frac{1}{2}$ hours according to size. The bird is then delicious to eat and the stock may be kept for future use.

Chicken stock with rather less flavor but still with useful "body" may be made by smashing the bones of a chicken carcass and putting them, together with any remaining meat, into a pan with vegetables, herbs and seasonings, as described above. Simmer steadily for 2–3 hours.

In all cases, strain stock into a bowl and, when cold, remove the fat (which is good for cooking: heat it gently for some time to boil off the moisture before attempting to use it for frying, but it may be used as is for sauces etc.).

**Note** Both chicken and veal stocks make a rich and useful aspic jelly. If your stock is still liquid when cold, reheat and simmer uncovered until reduced by a third or a half.

# Fond Brun

## BROWN STOCK

Proceed as for *fond blanc* but, after blanching, place the drained veal bones in a greased roasting pan. Cook in a preheated 425°F oven for about 40 minutes, turning occasionally, until evenly browned. Put the browned bones in a large pan and proceed as for *fond blanc*. If the roasting pan contains brown juices, *déglacer* it with a little of the water and add to the stock pan.

## MEAT JELLY

Used as a meat glaze or to add flavor and gloss to sauces, this is simply a *fond brun* which you continue simmering, uncovered, until it reduces to a thick syrup. Stir and skim from time to time.

# Court Bouillon/ Fumet de Poisson

## FISH STOCK
### YIELD APPROX. 1 QUART

Ask your fish merchant for fish trimmings (heads, tails and fins, skin, bones).

Rinse $2\frac{1}{4}$ lbs fish trimmings and put in a large pan with a sliced onion, 2 sliced carrots, 1–2 chopped celery stalks, a crushed garlic clove (optional), a sprig of thyme, 2–3 bay leaves, several sprigs of parsley (or a bouquet garni in lieu of the last 3 items), salt and black pepper. Cover with 3 cups water and 1 cup dry white wine. (The proportion of wine to water may be adjusted to suit you; dry hard cider is perfectly acceptable, as is dry vermouth. In some circumstances red wine or rosé may be used instead.)

Bring to a boil and simmer until reduced by one-third (about 20–30 minutes). Strain well.

## CLARIFIED STOCK

When meat or fish has been cooked in stock, the stock may become slightly opaque. If it is to be used for aspic or as a glaze, or even if you want a nice clear gravy, it is easily cleared thus.

Measure the cold stock and strain it into a clean pan. In a bowl, beat to a light froth 1–2 egg whites for each quart of stock (add the crushed shells too if liked). Heat the stock and slowly add the whites, whisking "in reverse" (pushing the froth into the liquid rather than lifting the liquid up) until it boils and a thick froth covers the top. Stop whisking, lower the heat as far as possible and allow to simmer very gently (liquid should barely tremble so as not to break up the "crust") for up to 1 hour. Allow to settle.

Scald some cheesecloth, wring it out and lay it, doubled, in a strainer over a clean bowl. Pour the stock carefully through the cloth, holding back the frothy crust until last. If the stock is insufficiently cleared, place the strainer over another bowl and pour the stock through the cloth (*and crust*) again.

# DOUGHS AND PASTRIES

## Pâte à Pain

### BASIC WHITE BREAD

1 *cake* (0.6 oz) *compressed yeast*
1 tsp *sugar*
*about* 2 cups *warm water*
6 cups *bread flour*
1 tbsp *salt*

Cream the yeast and sugar with about one third of the water; leave in a warm place to froth up.

Sift the flour and salt into a warm bowl, make a well in the flour and pour in the yeast mixture. Stir, gradually pulling in the flour from the sides; add more water as you go, working with your hand until you have a soft dough. Knead for about 10 minutes on a floured board. Cover with a cloth (or put in an oiled plastic bag) and leave in a warm place to rise. It should ideally double in size – the time taken will depend on the temperature, but don't try to hurry it.

On a floured board punch down the dough, then knead it again for 5 minutes or until smooth and elastic. Divide in half and put into greased pans; leave to rise in a warm place until dough rises to the tops of the pans.

Bake in a preheated 400°F oven. Take one loaf out after 45 minutes and tap the base; if it sounds solid, put both back without their pans and, if top is not nicely browned, turn up the oven very slightly. Tap again after a further 10 minutes; the bread is ready when it sounds hollow.

Leave to cool before slicing – if you possibly can!

## Pâte Feuilletée

### PUFF PASTRY

There are many different methods for making this feather-light pastry, and they all require care. It is important that the butter be of the correct consistency (see recipe), and my advice would be to take it from the refrigerator just long enough before you start so that a quick press with a knuckle makes a good dent without leaving an oily patch. The method given here is, strictly speaking, a combination of those normally thought of as "puff" and "flaky" pastries.

Don't make this pastry if you or the kitchen are very hot; in very warm weather it's advisable to rest the pastry dough in the refrigerator.

(Unless you are trying to advance your reputation as a pastrycook, commercial brands of puff pastry are adequate for most purposes.)

1½ cups *flour*
*pinch of salt*
¾ cup *butter*
1–2 tsp *lemon juice (optional)*
*up to* 1 cup *iced water*

Sift the flour and salt into a bowl. Take a quarter of the butter and cut it into the flour with a pastry blender. When the pieces are fairly small and well coated with flour, rub them into the flour by picking the mixture up with the fingertips and rubbing lightly so that it falls back into the bowl. Do this quickly and gently until fat is barely distinguishable from flour.

Now add the lemon juice, followed by the iced water, a little at a time (you may not need it all). Mix quickly – first with the knife, then the fingers – until you have a soft but firm dough. Roll it out to a rectangle about 1 inch thick.

Take the remaining butter and beat it if necessary to get it as nearly as possible the same consistency as the dough. Shape it into a flat brick and place it on the dough about one-third of the way along; fold the dough over it towards you and lightly seal edges. Leave to rest in a cool place 15 minutes.

Roll quickly and lightly, towards the fold and then back. Give dough a half turn, fold it in three and roll again; rest 15 minutes. Continue resting and rolling thus six times in all. (If streaks of butter still show, roll once more.) Rest 15 minutes in a cool place before use. If it's not to be used for several hours, wrap it in a clean cloth.

## Pâte Brisée

### PIE PASTRY

Made the French way. In the U.S. it is usual to rub the fat into the flour before mixing in the other ingredients. As far as I know, any differences between these methods are virtually undetectable in the final pastry.

These quantities should give enough pastry to line a 10 inch tart pan or two 7 inch ones.

1¾ cups *flour*
¾ tsp *salt*
½ cup *softened butter*
1 *egg or 2 yolks*
*about* ¼ cup *cold water*

Sift the flour onto a marble slab or counter top. Make a well in the center and add the salt, butter and egg. Stir these in with the fingertips, gradually drawing in the flour from the sides. When at least two-thirds of the flour is incorporated, add some of the water if it seems necessary. You want to finish with an easily malleable ball of dough which is dry to the touch. The trick is to add the liquid very cautiously – using less, or occasionally more, than is given in the recipe. It is difficult to correct a dough which is sticky or too hard without spoiling it.

Chill for 30 minutes before using.

According to use, different fats – or a combination of fats – may be substituted for the butter; some recipes even call for oil.

A richer pastry (shorter, lighter and more fragile) may be achieved by increasing the proportion of fat to flour. If necessary some of the egg may be replaced with cold water.

For *Pâte Sucrée* (a sweet pastry suitable for fruit tarts etc.), 3 tbsp or more sugar may be added to the above ingredients. It may also be flavored with vanilla, orange or lemon rind, lemon juice and so on. In some cases, about one-third of the flour may be replaced with ground almonds.

For a savory pastry, pepper may be added as well as salt. Grated cheese may also be incorporated (if the cheese is very fatty, and if a very light pastry is unsuitable, reduce the fat slightly).

# Pâte à Choux

## CHOUX PASTRY

¾ cup *water*
5 tbsp *butter*
½ tsp *salt*
1 cup *flour*
3–4 eggs, *according to size*
grated rind of 1 *lemon*
1–2 tsp *orange-flower water*

Put the water, butter and salt into a pan over very low heat. Meanwhile sift the flour onto a piece of paper and beat one of the eggs in a small bowl to mix it thoroughly.

When the butter is melted, bring the liquid to a boil and take from heat. Immediately add all the flour at once and beat vigorously, just long enough to make a smooth paste that holds its shape and pulls away from the sides of the pan.

Add the unbeaten eggs, one at a time, beating vigorously between each to incorporate completely. If necessary add just enough of the last (beaten) egg to make a heavy, shiny paste. Add flavorings as required and bake according to your recipe.

### To Bake "Blind"

Baking a pastry case without a filling – e.g. for fresh fruit tarts. Pie pastry (*pâte brisée* or *pâte sucrée*) is usually used.

Line the flan ring or tart pan with pastry dough and press in gently but firmly. Prick the bottom with a fork, line the pastry with foil or parchment paper and fill with dried beans, pottery beads, rice or lentils etc. These can be kept to use again and again for this purpose. Make sure the sides are well supported to prevent them collapsing during cooking. Bake in a preheated 400°F oven *(pâte brisée)* or 375°F *(pâte sucrée)* (unless otherwise instructed).

Remove after 15 minutes if the tart is to be put back in the oven at a later time. If a cold uncooked filling is to be used, bake for 15 minutes; remove the foil and beans and continue baking for 5–10 minutes longer or until the pastry is firm and golden. Allow to cool completely before filling.

RIGHT *Massive loaves of pain de campagne*

# PREPARATION

## To Prepare Mussels (and Clams)

Wash the mussels in several changes of cold water, brushing off all traces of sand or mud; pull off as much weed as you can. Discard any mussels which remain open when you handle them.

In the absence of any instructions in your recipe, open the mussels by putting them in a pan with a little water and shaking them gently over a brisk heat. Depending on the quantity, all the shells should open in 1–2 minutes; discard any which do not. Remove any further weed or other "foreign bodies" remaining inside.

Strain the cooking liquid through a fine cloth and keep it to use in any accompanying sauce.

## To Prepare Squid

Wash the squid well. Grasp the body in one hand and the head in the other and pull them apart; the transparent blade "bone" and most of the intestines will come away with the head section. Detach these and throw them away. Check that no blade remains in the pocket and turn the latter inside out to clean it thoroughly. Turn it back right way out and remove the mottled membranous skin (once torn, this comes away quite easily). Leave squid in cold water until you're ready to use them.

Remove any ink bags from the sides of the head and the horny bit in the center of the tentacles. Wash again, after which the tentacles and any flesh on the head may be chopped to use as instructed in your recipe.

BELOW *Fishing nets in a Mediterranean port*

## To Peel Chestnuts

Nick the brown shells with a sharp knife. Cover with cold water and bring quickly to a boil; remove from heat. Take 2 or 3 nuts from the pan at a time and, as quickly as possible (they're very hot to handle), pare off both the hard and the soft inner skins.

If you are peeling a large quantity, you'll need to bring the water back to a boil from time to time.

## To Cook Chestnuts

If your recipe doesn't suggest otherwise, simply put the peeled chestnuts into boiling water to cover, bring back to a boil and simmer until tender. According to the size, ripeness and freshness of the chestnuts, this may take anything from 20 to 40 minutes, usually around 25–30; test with a skewer.

# Glossary of Cooking Terms

**Bouillon**
Broth; meat, vegetable or fish stock.

**Bouquet Garni**
Bunch of herbs, bound with string or tied in small squares of cheesecloth, used for flavoring soups, stews or *court bouillon*. Traditionally the herbs are two or three parsley sprigs, a sprig of thyme and a bay leaf, but celery leaves, marjoram, rosemary and savory etc. can also be included.

**Croûtes**
Slices of fried or toasted bread, sometimes spread with a savory mixture, served as a garnish.

**Croûtons**
Small cubes or pieces of fried or toasted bread, generally served with cream or puréed soups. For garlic croûtons the bread is fried in garlic butter, or a cut garlic clove is rubbed over the bread after toasting.

**Déglacer**
To dilute the sediment and juices in a roasting dish or frying pan with a specified liquid (e.g. wine, stock or cream) to enrich a sauce or gravy.

**Flamber**
To set light to warmed wine or spirit. This burns out the alchohol and improves the flavor of the food to which it is then added.

**Hachis**
Literally chopped. A forcemeat of meat, herbs, vegetables etc.

**Larding**
To prevent very lean cuts of meat from drying out during cooking, fat is added thus: using a larding needle threaded with thin strips of pork fat, sew rows of stitches into the meat about 1 inch long, cutting the fat just above the surface between each stitch.

**Liaison**
Mixture for thickening and binding sauces, gravies and soups. The most common are a flour and butter roux, kneaded butter or egg yolks and cream.

**Persillade**
Sprinkling of finely chopped parsley, often mixed with bread crumbs and/or chopped garlic. Sometimes a parsley vinaigrette★.

**Roux**
Mixture of fat and flour which when cooked is used as a base for savory sauces.

**Zest**
Outer rind of citrus fruits containing the essential oils.

# Acknowledgments

Many individuals have helped us with this book: chefs both famous and unknown, and a small army of housewives – friends, landladies and casual acquaintances. We found a number of hints and a lot of information in old cookbooks, particularly the *Livre de Cuisine* I mentioned in the Introduction and *La Cuisinière Provençale* (Tacussel, Marseille, 1895).

We should particularly like to thank the following for their more extensive help (addresses in parentheses indicate that our friends are no longer there):

Emile Arcé, Hôtel du Trinquet, St Etienne de Baïgorry

Noël Arin, Auberge de Kérank, Plouharnel

Jacques Billet, Moulin des Ferrières, nr. Lourdes

Georges Blanc, Chez la Mère Blanc, Vonnas

David Bouviala, Hostellerie du Lévézou, Salles-Curan

Mme Paulette Bouyssou, Tursac

Mme José Brou, Creissels, Millau

Mme Jeannine Cabourg, Hôtel Angleterre et Cheval Blanc, Bernay

Louis Chanuet (Hôtel Moderne, Cluny)

Michel Dauven, Auberge du Soir, Brantôme

M. and Mme Dauzen, le Château, Bourdeilles

Jean-François and Yves Decuq, Hôtel Moderne et Gare, St-Affrique

Editions René Dessagne, Limoges

Jean-Michel Flavin (Restaurant au Marais, Coulon)

Michel Garrigou, Hôtel St-Albert, Sarlat

Mme Guiraud, Montdragon

Maurice Isabal, Hôtel Ithurria, Aïnhoa

The late M. Lacombe (Hôtel Pradel, St Etienne Cantalès)

M. and Mme Georges Lassaques, Château des Pauvres, Sarlat

M. et Mme Leysalles, Hotel Cro-Magnon, Les Eyzies

Mme Mazeau, la Bergerie, Château-l'Evêque

Marc Meneau, l'Espérance, St-Père, Vézelay

Jean-Pierre Michel, La Regalido, Fontvieille

Jean-Marie Miquel, Oustal del Barry, Najac

Gabriel Rousselet and Marcel Roure, Les Bories, Gordes

Julien Savy, Hôtel Moderne, Rodez

Syndicat d'Initiative, St-Girons

G. Thibaut, Ostellerie de Vieux Pérouges, Pérouges

Above all, our thanks are due to the anonymous French country wife through the ages, from whose ingenuity all the recipes have evolved.

Color photographs by Denis Hughes-Gilbey except for those on the following pages which are by Fred Mancini; 21, 23 top, 25, 26, 31, 36 top, 37, 38, 39, 40, 42, 46, 50, 53, 54, 56, 57, 58, 61, 64, 65, 66, 70, 73, 74 top, 76, 83, 84, 85, 92, 93, 95, 103, 104 top, 106, 114, 117, 118, 121, 124, 125, 126, 129

Edited by Lucy Shankleman
Designed by Patrick Frean and Joyce Chester
Black and white illustrations by Hannah Firmin
Preparation of food for photography by Heather Lambert, Janice Murfitt and Ann Hughes-Gilbey
Text adapted for U.S. publication by Norma MacMillan

The publishers would like to thank Divertimenti, 68 Marylebone Lane, London W1 for the generous loan of some of the tableware used in photography.
The publishers are also grateful to Amélie and Louis Bertoni for kindly allowing us to use their home for photography.

# Index